The Online Business Academy for ChatGPT

How to Start, Stay Ahead of the Game, and Scale a Side Hustle of Passive Income to 10k by Using the Ever-changing, Yet Profound AI Algorithm

Written By:

Thomas Bourne

i

Table Of Contents

Introduction

Picture this,

It's the 1st of January, and you're taking stock of how the previous year went for you. You take a deep breath and think of how much your life improved because you picked up this book, read it earnestly, and decided to apply what you've learned immediately after reading. You remember that this book promised to show you how to earn up to $10k with a passive side hustle. You wince a little as you recall how doubtful you were when you started reading, but you also admit that you were very persistent and determined to succeed with this book. And succeed, you did.

You check your account balance on your phone and remember how you had to skip some meals just to meet up with your bills or make do with ramen some nights to get by. You realize that you've really managed to make a crazy amount of money in a post-pandemic economy that had all the professors and think tanks predicting a financial Armageddon. You smile and send a heartfelt thank-you to your past self, the one that had the courage to buy this book and implement it ruthlessly. Then you put your pen to paper and write your financial goals for the new year (hint; it's about 7 to 8 figures), unafraid because you know you've equipped yourself with the right knowledge to achieve all your goals and more.

If you're still with me and didn't scoff or roll your eyes even once when you read that last paragraph, welcome; you're in the right place. You're the kind of person who believes they can achieve whatever they set their minds to and that nothing is ever out of reach for them if they dare to dream. I daresay that with your grit and mindset, you're right on track to getting everything you've ever wanted.

It's perfectly normal to scoff at the first part of this introduction, especially if you've never paid much attention to passive income or the idea of side hustles. I mean, the biggest hurdle you'll have to face on your journey to $10k is that you may not believe it's possible for you to achieve it. The good news is that once you've conquered that mindset, put in the work, and started implementing what you've learned here, you'll definitely see results. So I'd like to ask you for the benefit of the doubt, an open mind, and the willingness to do the work. Do we have a deal?

I'm positive that you've at least heard about ChatGPT, and you know what it does. You may have even heard that AI is the future and will make humans obsolete by taking our jobs. All you have to do is get on social media to hear about how people are utilizing AI and, more importantly, ChatGPT in their various fields. I think we can both agree that there's a lot of noise out there, which can be more than a little confusing. I've learned that an overload of information leads to analysis paralysis—that state where you have so much info that you don't know what to do with it. Trust me; it's not a lot of fun. That's where this book comes in to rescue you.

Let's talk a bit about you, shall we? You probably already have some source of income and are looking for a way to add more income streams to what you already have. Or you may not even have a business yet and would like to take charge of your finances and start to earn well. You've probably heard a lot about AI but don't know how to use it to make money. You may even feel like getting into AI may be too stressful because your current business takes a lot of your time, as it is. Most importantly, you're uber-focused on becoming sustainably wealthy, developing your personal finance, investing, and earning your way to long-term financial security. In essence, you're ready and willing to change your life by creating a passive income stream through Artificial Intelligence.

I'd like you to see this book as a journey. It has been created and formulated with you in mind. It'll take you from the basics of AI, everything you need to know, to the practical aspects of getting cool cash into your account every month. You'll learn creative strategies and tips for building a side hustle tailored to your personality and skills. You don't have to do what everyone else on social media is doing to make money if that's not your speed. You'll see how to use AI to start a business that compliments you and reflects your strong qualities.

The journey starts with understanding exactly what Artificial Intelligence is and how it came to be. I mean, we can't claim to know the important facts about anything if we don't know exactly how it started, right? Perfect. The first part of this book will deal with the nitty-gritty of AI technology you need to know about. You'll learn how it's applied to make life easier in different industries. The idea here is to help you see how there are no borders regarding the various ways AI can be used. You'll open your mind and adopt a problem-solving mentality that may even see you creating the next wildfire AI that could solve a major need and become an overnight sensation worldwide. Needless to say, that would also make you an overnight billionaire. If that happens, I guess we can conclude that this book has over-delivered on its promise, yes? The possibilities are endless, my friend, and I can't wait to see how you'll take advantage of it.

Next, we'll hop on the famous and somewhat crowded ChatGPT train to see what it's all about. You'll learn about the crazy potentials ChatGPT presents to you and its limitations.

You'll learn how to master the interface and see how it can be used. Having your own ChatGPT set up without knowing how to use the prompts is like Aladdin getting stuck outside the cave full of treasures without knowing the password. We definitely do not want that. You'll learn how to speak to your ChatGPT to get the best results from it. I'll give you a little secret, knowing how to use the right prompts can differentiate your results from another user's. The best outcome goes to the person who knows how to use prompts correctly. That's what we will learn in the first part of this book. In fact, with the value you've gained from this part alone, you can make a decent living by teaching others how to use prompts for the best results. Yep. When I promised to give you the most bang for your buck, I wasn't kidding.

You'll see how to go beyond ChatGPT to improve your business. You'll learn how to apply AI to whatever you've already got going on and how to make it better. Can AI help you make money off real estate investing? Can it help you make a killing on the stock market and eliminate the risk of investing in the wrong kind of stocks? What about the oh-so-scary crypto market? Can AI help you make a healthy profit without getting scalped? You'll learn all these and more here.

If you're thinking that you don't know how to set up a business or that your current business isn't even doing so great, hold on to your horses because help is here. In the second part of this book, you'll learn how to choose the best type of side hustle to start, how to find people to buy what you're selling, how to find out if people are indeed willing to buy what you're selling and how to create the right product to fit your target market. You'll see the best way to build your website, build your social media presence and create the right content to ensure that you get sold out back-to-back. Wanna know the beautiful thing about all this? You'll get to use AI to do everything without breaking a sweat. If that isn't a sweet deal, I don't know what is.

The AI industry moves fast and you'll lose out if you're caught snoozing. You'll learn how to follow the latest updates and trends. You'll see how to take advantage of these findings to make more money or better position your brand as an authority, eventually leading to more sales. You'll see how to grow your business so you're not stuck making the same amount of money every month. Instead, you'll learn how to jack up your earnings and different ways to make even more money from what you already have. You'll understand how to market effectively with AI and how to set it up such that you don't even have to be in front of your screen 24/7 before your money comes in.

What if things go bust with your business? What if your customers have an issue with your product or services? How do you manage your money and budget to keep your business running? What if the AI industry changes? How can you adapt? Should you think about ethical, legal, and technical issues? Is there a way to ensure that this business keeps generating an income year in and year out? You'll see exactly how to build a sustainable, income-generating business with AI with all your possible questions answered and all niggling doubts satisfied.

Running a successful AI-based business is all about taking action as quickly as possible, so I suggest you dive right into the first part of this book and get started! All I'll ask is that you let me know how your journey is going via email or by dropping a comment right here on Amazon.

Cheers to making as much money as possible this year!

PART ONE

Whenever I start something new or choose to do something a bit risky, I always start by modulating my mindset. I believe that success starts from the mind, and I never hesitate to take advantage of that principle by priming my mind for what I'm about to embark on. This may sound like some hocus-pocus but trust me, it works! Plus, there's nothing weird or woo-woo about it. It's just slowing down and intentionally connecting with your mind to get it in the best shape to receive and use information well.

Let's do a little exercise together, shall we? First, I want you to pause and close your eyes. Take five deep breaths and hold them for five seconds before exhaling. Then, try to clear your mind of thoughts while mentally scanning each part of your body for tension. If you notice that any parts are tense, like your neck, shoulders, or your stomach, for example, consciously work on relaxing them as you keep breathing in and out gently. You can do this while standing, but sitting or relaxing may be best. You can also do this in a crowded or noisy place, but if you can find a quiet corner, please do.

After relaxing the tense parts of your body and trying to clear your mind, think about what you're about to learn. Examine any resistance or objections your mind may have and quietly shoot them down. Tell yourself you'll do your best and get the best out of your efforts. Accustom your mind to how much money you want to make and visualize that amount sitting pretty in your account. Keep breathing and preparing yourself for this change while encouraging only positive, restful, victorious thoughts. This can take as much as 15 minutes or even an hour if you're up for it. It can also be done in five minutes if you don't have much time. The aim is to start doing it, get used to it, and do it as many times as possible throughout your journey. Do we have a deal?

This first part is all about introducing you to the concept of Artificial Intelligence as it really is. What is it really, and what was it developed for? Where did it start? Many people have many things to say about AI as it is today, but you'll be surprised to learn that it's been around for a lot longer than you can imagine. In fact, I daresay that you've interacted with AI in numerous ways by now. In this first part, we'll learn about the types of AI, what they do, and how they can be used.

Have you heard of or interacted with an AI chatbot before? You probably have, and you'll see the different types of chat and which is best for your side hustle plans. You also have some burning questions about AI and the future. Like me, you may have wondered if the producers of the movie *Terminator* were on to something, and the advent of AI will end in flames and tears as the world burns down while an unblinking red eye stares at you. Or perhaps *The Matrix* may be a more accurate prediction of the future of AI, as far as you're concerned. Trust me, those are very valid fears, and they may even be a stumbling block to getting into the AI industry. Not to worry, we'll dismantle all those fears and answer all the questions you may have.

Wondering why you'll learn so much about chatbots? It's because our MVP, ChatGPT is a chatbot that's the key to your success. By the time you're done with the second chapter, you'll know everything there is to know about it and how to use it to make more money from the comfort of your room. Or maybe from the shores of The Maldives while you're on holiday.

You'll learn the basics of AI prompts such that even if a fancy new AI is on the block, you'll still be confident enough to handle it, no matter what. You'll see all the things you can do with ChatGPT as well as the things you probably shouldn't do with it. You'll know where to let the AI lead and where to add that much-needed human element to your business.

Ultimately, you'll have achieved a distinct blend of automation with a wide streak of empathy and accessibility that'll set your business apart from others in the industry. You'll learn how to combine your chatbot with other services to create a holistic experience for your potential clients.

Ready to jump in?

Chapter One

The Ai Guide

"Some people call this artificial intelligence, but the reality is this technology will enhance us. So instead of artificial intelligence, I think we'll augment our intelligence."
– Ginni Rometty

When you hear AI, what immediately comes to mind? If you asked someone about it twenty-five years ago, they would have told you about some massive supercomputers that had to be housed in large rooms with large fans to keep them cool. Back then, the most amazing thing these machines could do was converse with humans within set guidelines. When Hollywood put their own spin on it, movies like *The Matrix* and *Terminator* were born. If the AI enthusiasts of old could see how far the technology has advanced now, they'd be convinced that the Hollywood writers were on to something with those movies. Could they ever have imagined how far we've come? As crazy as it sounds, I absolutely think they looked forward to days like this, and it's up to you to take advantage of this era.

Like my friend Drew wrote in a recent email to me, "It feels almost criminal not to take advantage of the opportunities that are right in front of us." I can't help agreeing wholeheartedly. Let's see what AI is really about, shall we?

Artificial Intelligence: The Technology of Ease

I'd like to think that Artificial Intelligence technology was born out of a desire to maximize efforts while minimizing costs. The main idea is centered around increasing productivity as much as possible.

As we go along on this journey, you'll realize that you've interacted with AI in one form or another, and you'll definitely do some more interacting, even if you don't choose to practice what you'll learn here. The great part is that it's been applied across multiple industries, and every day, new frontiers are crossed in the march to make life easier for man. I guess we could say that the point of AI is to keep us sipping colorful cocktails at some beach in a tropical location while getting all the hard, boring stuff done. I'd definitely go for a deal like that.

Artificial intelligence has successfully:

- Created a means to provide us with important information at the speed of light.

- Transform the way we communicate with family, friends, and clients.

- Automated the repetitive, boring tasks that must be carried out daily in business and across many industries.

- Provided new ways for us to relax and enjoy our leisure time.

- Improved our society's security and boosted our sense of safety.

- Increased productivity in the different aspects of life and made our processes more efficient.

- Empowered us to make smarter decisions every day based on well-analyzed data.

- Given us more avenues to express our creative and innovative side (Bashar, 2023).

You may not realize, but incorporating AI into the everyday workings of their businesses has resulted in a drastic reduction in the cost of production. According to Tech see, AI has saved about $68 billion dollars in costs in the customer care industry alone (TechSee, 2018). If we were to pull similar figures for other industries, I'm sure we'd see a similar trend there.

Let's bring it down to a personal level now. What if you had to go to work tomorrow and you realized you'd probably spend a lot of time outdoors because you had a lot of meetings. You'd want to know how the weather turns out tomorrow. Is it going to rain, or will there be a snowstorm? Or will it be bright and sunny? Instead of going to your weather app to check it out for yourself, all you'd have to do is ask Siri or Alexa about the next day's weather forecast. Siri tells you that it will be a rainy day with estimated rainfall times. That's pretty great, right? Then, Siri takes things one step further and suggests that she sets an alarm to remind you to take your umbrella before you leave for work. How useful would that be, knowing that you don't have to sweat the small stuff like that anymore? That's the beauty of AI for you.

Or perhaps, you have the cutest doggo ever, but you have to leave him at home all day while you're at work. Wouldn't you feel better knowing that you can always check on him from the comfort of your workplace? You could monitor his movements and even be heard by your pet when he wanders too close to an unsafe area. How cool would that be?

If we head over to the agricultural sector, AI has gotten so advanced that it can tell the farmer about the weather, the state of the soil, and whether the seed to be planted is good or bad (Appen).

Machine learning is an area of AI that we'll take a closer look at quite soon. It's all about how artificial intelligence learns about human behavior simply to understand it better and make life easier for us (Gardener, 2019). For example, it'll help us monitor our households, recommend the right type of groceries to buy, based on existing health conditions, and even order new supplies when the fridge is running low!

The bottom line is that AI exists to make your life more organized, free up your time so you can do more stuff that makes you happy, help you be happier too, and improve your life's quality in the long run (Rossow, 2018).

Now you know exactly why people keep pushing for newer and more efficient versions of this tool to make your life better and ultimately help you earn more. Who would you rather be in this scenario? Would you prefer to fold your hands and let this opportunity and its juicy benefits pass you by? Wouldn't you rather take advantage of this era to make the most of it?

Brief History of AI

It'll be amiss of us to dive straight into learning about ChatGPT without first understanding how it came to be and the basic principle behind the technology. So let's take a brief walk down memory lane to see how AI came to be in the first place.

What does Artificial Intelligence mean anyway? The plain and simple concept involves having software that attempts to copy the human brain such that it can think like a human being. An intelligent copycat of the human brain if you will. The term 'Artificial Intelligence' was first devised by John McCarthy, who was doing a lot of work on that scene and even had the first AI conference. This started as far back as 1956 when the term was coined.

The industry was off to a great start, and soon after, Shakey, the first general-purpose mobile robot was created. It could understand its environment and behavior and think about its actions as opposed to other robots that would need specific instructions for every stage of a large task. Shakey could process commands and break them down into smaller chunks by itself. It was developed at the Artificial Intelligence Center of the Stanford Research Institute from 1966 to 1972 *(Wikipedia).*

Greatly encouraged, work continued, and by 1996, a chess-playing computer lost a chess match against the world chess champion, Kasparov. But by 1997, Deep Blue, the same computer, defeated Kasparov in a six-game re-match after getting upgraded. It was the first computer to win such a match against a world champion (Kelley, 2023).

It wasn't all rosy in the industry because there were periods of 'AI winter' where research and development in the industry stopped. The first winter period was in the 1970s, but it kicked off again in the 1980s, majorly because the world superpowers were in a race to develop the best AI. The result of the reawakening gave birth to expert systems, which were able to ask questions, solve problems and offer solutions in seconds, just like Deep Blue. The second AI winter was from 1987 to 1993, when the expert systems became too expensive to maintain and update.

Natural Language Processing (NLP) was developed to help computers understand human language in the 1960s and has been developed ever since. AI bots came on the scene in the early 1990s, and they could retrieve news from the internet, browse the web and perform simple actions. These were the forbears of advanced Chatbots like ChatGPT and other virtual assistance bots.

Machine learning (ML) was also used to develop NLP for AI. It taught AI to make decisions without being specifically programmed to make those moves. One fun fact to know is that this concept was created to mimic how brain cells interact (Foote, 2002).

By 2002, the first robotic vacuum cleaners were produced, which practically heralded the industry's rapid development. By 2005, speech recognition, facial recognition, and dancing robots had started gaining ground. By 2011, Siri and Alexa began to become popular and experienced rapid upgrades and iterations. Big companies like Facebook started using facial recognition and integrating it into their algorithm. That's why Facebook was so eerily accurate in recognizing faces in several photos. At this point, AI was so good that it could differentiate between identical twins! In 2011, another AI, Watson, won Jeopardy, the popular game show.

Can we talk about Artificial Intelligence without mentioning Alan Turing? I think not. Alan Turing is one of the more popular founding fathers of artificial intelligence. He was a British mathematician and logician who made significant contributions to mathematical logic, philosophy, computer science, artificial intelligence, and artificial life. He was a major supporter of the idea that the human brain operates like a computer. He argued that the brain's cortex could be likened to an unorganized machine that becomes organized through training (Encyclopedia Britannica). He was so passionate about the idea that he created the Turing test, formulated to test a machine's ability to think and act intelligently, like a human being. The test has been upheld as a way to qualify and classify AI, even today. Of course, it's also been highly criticized. Interestingly, the emergence of ChatGPT restarted the discussion, and some people agree that it has successfully met the Turing criteria.

It's been a long journey, and thanks to rapid innovation, it's moving fast. I hope you're ready to jump on and hang on for the ride!

Applications of AI

AI has been used by a lot of industries in different ways. Take a second to think about it; what's the coolest application of AI for you? For me, I'd have to say that it's possible for wearable devices to constantly monitor your blood pressure and other vital signs on the go. It doesn't stop there. If, for example, someone had a heart attack or they lost consciousness, the AI is potentially able to detect that, call for help from the nearest healthcare facility and guide the paramedics to the unconscious person's location. The technology may not exist yet, but I think it is close. Another great application of AI that I think is fantastic is that it has been used to develop vaccines and cures for conditions much faster than humans would have been capable of.

So, if I had to ask you, what would it be for you? I'm sure you're considering that it's a great way to make more money while doing less. If that's what's on your mind, I have no choice but to agree. AI is fantastic for business. I mean, I'm sure you have *some* idea of how handy it is, but trust me, by the time you're done with this book, you'll be floored by just how much you can do with AI. That sounds like a tall order, but it's absolutely achievable.

Before we talk about AI for your new passive income side hustle, let's take a second to appreciate how versatile it is. Here are some of the industries that use AI today and how they use it:

1. Astronomy

Since the dawn of time, man has always been drawn to the stars and the idea of other life forms out in the great big universe. Thanks to AI, we have been able to explore other planets and have a pretty good idea of what sort of gases, solids, and other substances are out there. I mean, if you haven't been living under a rock, you've probably heard about SpaceX which Mr Elon Musk owns. From the looks of things, Elon may just have plans to buy up the whole of Planet Mars and set up a new branch there. How has he been able to do so much out there? You're right, through AI.

2. Transport

If you've ever been to the airport or train station on a busy day, you'll appreciate the sheer magnitude of people traveling daily. Companies use artificial intelligence to fix transport prices, assist customers when booking tickets, calculate arrival and departure times, and even attend to customer queries online.

3. Travel

The next time you take a summer trip or plan a getaway somewhere by a lake or up in the mountains, think about how you can book your Airbnb, plan your trips, and book your hotels. Do a few helpful apps come to mind? You bet! A large part of this is driven by AI, and in the years to come, we'll see more and more innovations like this.

4. Healthcare

Apart from the fact that AI is used to develop vaccines and stuff like that, it's also why your hospital visits aren't longer than they currently are, for the most part. It's been used to do stuff like record patient data, file and store the data, measure important stats like blood pressure, analyze blood work, analyze genes, and other amazing things. Let's not forget the wearable devices like your smartwatches and others.

5. Social media

How can Facebook, Instagram, or TikTok store and manage so many profiles? Why can you save posts or bookmark threads and still find them when needed? How can these social media platforms recommend your friends and family to you on their apps?

AI has been widely used in social media, and with the advent of Virtual Reality, it looks like it's only about to get better.

6. Business operations, marketing, and customer service

E-commerce platforms like Amazon, eBay, and Shopify use AI to optimize their user experience and drive more website sales. It's also used to recommend other items you'd want to get, advertise best-selling products, and receive feedback during shopping.

7. Surveillance and defense

AI has also been used for security purposes. This can go from as little as using your face to unlock your phone to as significant as tracking down criminals simply because a random street camera picked up their faces from the feed.

If we had to look at the different ways that Artificial intelligence can be used in the world today, we may need to take out a whole library to accommodate all the books we'd have to write. I hope you can see that the possibilities are endless for you, and that you can even think up new ways to use AI to solve everyday problems. Thanks to, well, AI, you don't need to have an extensive knowledge of coding or stuff like that to make your own tool.

Brief Explanation of AI Chatbots and Their Role

If you're wondering why we are paying a lot of attention to

Chatbots, it's because the main AI we'll be using to get you to $10k a month is a Chatbot. Also, Forbes predicted the Chatbot market will grow to $1.25 billion by 2025 (Patel, 2023). I'm not sure what you're thinking, but I definitely know that I'd like a slice of that pie. Wouldn't you?

A Chatbot is an AI-based program designed to simulate human conversation. In a nutshell, it can interpret user requests, process them, and give prompt yet relevant answers. A chatbot can identify exactly what a user needs, extract the useful information needed to assist the user, process it and give an accurate response.

Chatbots use a pattern-matching technique to group text together and study the grouped text patterns with AI Markup Language (AIML). They also use Natural Language Understanding (NLU) to convert text into data easier for the machine to understand. NLP also converts speech or text to data, making it clear to the AI.

The great thing about Chatbots is that they can either be simple or complex, which is based on how they've been designed. Like we saw in the history of AI, Chatbots evolved from the simple ones that could only answer Yes/No questions to the more advanced types like ChatGPT.

I'm pretty sure you've heard many people speculate about how AI is here to take human jobs and put them out of commission, and with the way these bots work, you'd be tempted to agree. Take this scenario, for example, you're up at night, trying to order something off a website. Suddenly, you put in card information and encounter a problem while trying to pay for your cart. What if it's 1 am on a Saturday, and the store doesn't open till 9 am Monday?

You would definitely want to speak to a customer care rep as soon as possible, right? Now if you owned the business, would you be amenable to paying extra to have a team member that's always available, 24/7? I mean, that's not even realistic.

Enter your chatbot. Using a chatbot allows you to receive some form of customer care as a customer and attend to your clients 24/7 as a business owner. Now, some of these bots can only connect you with a customer care agent who can speak to you and help out. Others can take your complaints and resolve them as best as they can. That's the beauty of a chatbot.

Basically, they can be programmed in two ways:

- Simple, rules-based bots that only do what they've been programmed to do.

- Decision-making/ AI bots that can learn beyond what it's been taught and are much better at conversation.

We'll get to this in a bit, but if you've interacted with any chatbot, I'd like you to try to classify them according to these two categories. For clarity's sake, a chatbot usually pops up at the bottom right corner of the screen with a message that offers to help you via chat. Sometimes they may be able to help you out by directing you to the relevant websites or showing you the right actions to take. Other times, they may only be able to connect you to an agent and tell you how long you'd have to wait. Some really innovative websites offer the options of games for you to play while you wait. In the next few sections, we will see the types of Chatbots and how they're used.

Types of AI Chatbots

For a while back there, it was amusing to see the Big Tech companies scramble to outdo themselves with their versions of AI Chatbots. You've probably watched many YouTube videos that tried to pit different types of AI against each other just to see which one was better. I don't think we can answer that question because new upgrades and updates are released every day. The entire industry is on its toes, and we're riding the crest of the AI wave. What a time to be alive!

From what we've discussed about chatbots in the previous sections, we've seen that they can perform various functions.

I may not have mentioned it explicitly before, but Alexa and Siri are chatbots too. If you've ever interacted with them, you'd have seen that the possibilities achieved with them are truly endless. Now just think about all the things you could do with ChatGPT. A whole lot more, let me tell you.

There are a lot of classification criteria for chatbots, but I'll show you a very simplified and comprehensive way to understand the different types of chatbots:

1. Rule-based/ Scripted /Quick reply chatbots

These bots are the most simplified version you'd find around these days. They only operate within a set of boundaries. These limits are determined by the rules guiding their interactions and actions. So this means that they can only answer simple questions and provide their users with a set of options that contain the most relevant answer for the user.

This kind of chatbot doesn't have a lot of room to learn or grow and cannot perform more complex operations outside its scope of use. They are great, but they could definitely be better. However, don't be too quick to underrate this type of bot because they still come in handy occasionally.

2. NLP/AI-driven, decision-making Chatbots

As the name implies, these Chatbots use Natural Language Processing to recognize sentence structure, interpret the text to data, process the request, and offer a relevant answer based on the gathered data. A significant characteristic here is the fact that this type of chatbot can learn from its previous experience to do better during future encounters. They may also be known as conversational Chatbots

3. Contextual/Context Enabled Chatbot

These Chatbots use Machine learning, AI and NLP to understand, learn and grow. They can convert text to data, group and process it, and extract relevant details! And provide answers based on the data they have. The great thing about this type of bot is that they can learn and grow from their past conversations to offer a better experience in the future.

These types of bots can be personalized to a specific user and can configure themselves to complement their user's needs based on their previous interactions, which they use to predict the future.

4. Voice-enabled chatbots

This category of chatbots takes things a step further, and they can decode voice commands and queries. They use text-to-speech as well as voice recognition APIs to respond to this.

5. Hybrid chatbots

These bots are a nice combination of Rule-based and AI

methodology such that you get to enjoy the benefits of both. This comes in handy because normal questions can be attended to with a capacity for learning and even taking action.

Understanding the difference between a chatbot and an AI virtual assistant is essential. A lot of people confuse one for the other, which is understandable because they are very similar. The main difference between both is their purpose and how they're designed. Chatbots are designed to do one specific thing, like attend to customers on a website or a social media platform, while VAs can perform different functions. AI like Siri, Alexa, and Cortana are examples of virtual assistants because they can do many things based on the user's needs.

Next up, we'll look at some use cases for chatbots.

Use Cases of AI Chatbots

Hold your horses there! If you're grimacing and wondering if you'll have to slug through fancy terms like 'use-case' all through the rest of this book, then you can and should relax because we're all about easy-to-understand concepts here, okay?

Use-case simply means 'example' or 'instance.' That's it. While I'm committed to giving you a seamless experience in the AI industry, you should start to familiarize yourself with terms like this. I mean, you'll be around here for a long time, so it's only right to get comfortable, don't you think?

Looking at the various use cases of AI chatbots is a great way to get even more familiar with the industry and start making those bucks. These chatbots are used in different ways; the key is picking the easiest way to understand it. To that end, we'll look at how their use cases are classified here:

1. By function

A handy way to consider the useful applications of chatbots is what they're used for. We already know that AI has a wide variety of functions, and we'll look at the specific uses here.

a) **Customer support:** this industry is perhaps one of the biggest and earliest beneficiaries of the AI wave via chatbots. A lot of companies started out using AI to attend to customers after hours when the staff was off duty. Organizations with a large customer base also use chatbots to sort and direct their customers to the appropriate departments to resolve their queries. These days chatbots can answer yes or no questions and even provide additional details when prompted. They are also used to find products, check inventory, verify order details, collect feedback, and offer solutions to customer complaints. They can also track the shipping process(Colm, 2022).

b) **Sales:** with how things are currently set up, chatbots generate more sales when customers shop online. It does this by recommending more products that complement what's already in the cart and suggesting offers that prompt you to buy more than you initially planned. I'll be honest, I've fallen for that once or twice, and I bet you have too.

c) **Marketing**: this is one of those use cases of chatbots that you should be especially interested in and that we'll discuss much later in the book. With the help of AI, they help to drive marketing efforts by personalizing copies to suit the customer and by showing content based on what they would like. Of course, this leads to a high sales conversion rate and better customer experience. If you've ever felt like everything you saw online while shopping seemed made for you, it probably was – by an AI chatbot.

What about finding new customers for a business? That's called generating leads, by the way, and this process has been simplified a lot, thanks to artificial intelligence. That means many organizations can get new potential customers for their brand and add them to an email list that is also chatbot coordinated.

d) **Employee assistance:** apart from helping out with customers, AI chatbots also help many busy employees stay on top of their schedules by reminding them about deadlines, scheduling meetings, and even doing mundane stuff like ordering office supplies (Freshchat, 2022).

These are the very important use cases for chatbots that you'll be taking advantage of to set up your own business. If you're not sold on their effectiveness, just look at Amtrak. They run trains between cities in the US and Canada and recorded a 25% increase in booking rates and a 50% increase in customer service and user engagement when they launched Julie, their chatbot. What's not to love about chatbots again?

2   By channel

We've seen some ways AI has been used for a seamless experience both on the customer-facing and employee-facing parts of the industry. Now let's see what channels they've been integrated into and utilized in:

a)   **Websites**: chatbots provide self-service options for customers, interact with users, and offer personalized suggestions for a better experience.

b)   **Social media apps**: Chatbots are also utilized on social media apps like Facebook, Twitter, and others.

c)   **Apps**: In-app bots have become quite popular, especially when you're trying to access the app creator's customer service.

These are not all the available use cases, but it's a great place to start. In the next section, we'll look at your burning questions about AI.

FAQs About AI

AI, as we know it, is here to stay, and we're all the better for it. The industry is fast evolving, but how can you stay current when you're still unclear on some basic concepts and ideas?

Exactly.

In this section, we'll look at the commonly asked questions about AI that you may have and how to answer them. Here are a few:

1. What is Artificial Intelligence (AI)?

Artificial Intelligence (AI) is a part of the study of computer science, which involves the research and development of intelligent machines that can think and work like humans. They use technologies like Natural Language Processing, speech recognition, deep learning, text analysis, and market recognition.

2. What can AI do?

There's a diverse range of applications for AI that we've already explored in previous sections. While self-driving cars haven't been perfected yet, AI can do other things like place phone calls, make appointments, answer customer queries, data analysis, and processing, and so on.

3. Can AI be potentially dangerous?

Yes, like every technological advancement, there's a potential for danger if the AI had control of critical human infrastructure like the power grid. It could also get hacked.

4. What are the advantages of AI?

The major advantage that makes AI so valuable is that it can process large amounts of data faster than humans. It can take this a step further and use this data to make mostly accurate predictions. This means it's good at tasks requiring keen attention to detail. This saves time, labor, and increases the overall productivity rate. Another huge plus is that you can rely on it always to give consistent results, and it doesn't need to take a day off.

5. What are the disadvantages of AI?

A current disadvantage of working with AI is that analyzing large amounts of data is quite expensive. Also, the recent advantages where AI can replicate voices, music, and faces and alter video clips create an opportunity for it to be used for the wrong purposes, bringing up many ethical concerns.

6. Will AI replace all human jobs in the future?

For sure, some jobs will be taken over by AI and rendered obsolete in the future, but that doesn't mean all human jobs will be taken over completely. There'll most likely be a higher demand for people trained to work with AI as well as faster job completion times. Partial or complete automation will also be a regular feature

As AI use opens up to involve more industries with limitless potential, it's up to people like you to take advantage of this opportunity now. You have nothing to lose!

Chapter Two

Before Using Chatgpt

"In a world where ChatGPT and other AI apps can do many things humans once needed to do themselves or needed to hire other humans to do, the question of 'how will I add value?' becomes more relevant than ever."
— Hendrith Vanlon Smith Jr.

My friend Ed had pretty much had it up to here. His whole life could be described as a series of bad days, or maybe bad years really. We talked about his problems a lot, and like most people, they had to do with money. He graduated from college with debt as usual and didn't get a great job until two years later. He got married, but unfortunately, his marriage ended after a couple of years, and he had to start paying for alimony. He made a couple of wrong choices, invested in some deals that he thought were legit until they crashed, and basically ended up in financial hot water. He found himself working three jobs, not sleeping well, not earning enough to pay his debts and have a life, or even enough to take a break for a while.

We talked about his situation a lot, and I persuaded him to start a side hustle with ChatGPT. He looked at me like I was slow and told me, "I barely have enough time to sleep or money to spend, and you think I need to start another job?!" I had to talk very fast to convince him, and when he settled down to listen to what I proposed, he reluctantly agreed and said that sleep was useless anyway.

Fast forward to the next four months after, I got an email from him, and he told me that he'd resigned from one of his jobs and stopped picking up overtime shifts. He was well on his way to regularly paying off his debt, and he'd started sleeping better. All because of AI. He said, *"I don't know why I didn't start this earlier, but I'm definitely making up for lost time!"*

ChatGPT: The AI-Powered Chatbot

I'd like to apologize in advance before you start this section. Yeah, I know it's strange but hear me out. You know how you attend a concert held by your favorite band, and there's that one person who won't stop fangirl-ing hard? You know what I mean, that person whose shrill scream manages to penetrate the din of the concert and they can be heard from the furthest reaches of the room.

That's going to be me with ChatGPT. Yep, sorry in advance. We're going to look at what makes this particular AI so special and why you should hop on this train to paradise. I will be cheesing quite hard, but I promise to bring you the facts. Deal?

Here's the fact, ChatGPT is the bomb diggity! No matter how anyone spins it, it's a big deal. To start with, it's a chatbot, just like we talked about earlier, but it goes quite a bit further than the other chatbots you may have heard about or used. The 'GPT' in its title stands for Generative Pre-trained Transformer, while the 'chat' part describes how it communicates with its users-via text.

It's a multi-purpose chatbot that uses AI and allows its users to put in a command, known as a 'prompt,' which it responds to. It's a Large Language Model, which simply means it was trained with massive data to help it generate accurate replies. It was developed by OpenAI, a tech startup currently taking the world by storm.

It was officially released in November 2022, but it's regularly updated, so new GPT models are available. ChatGPT is special because it's been trained to perform a variety of tasks which are then communicated via text. For example, you can't ask it to paint you a picture or sing a song (Shankland, 2023).

When first introduced, it was made available as a free version available for public use by anyone, anytime and anywhere. After a while, a paid version, ChatGPT Plus, was released. The best part is that with the paid version, you still get the same access you did with the free version, only you're promised faster response times, priority access when there's high demand and quick access to updates and new features. 24/7 customer service is also available for users of the paid version. It's currently billed at $20 per month, which is quite affordable, if you ask me.

The free version was a GPT - 3.5 model, but the latest model is the GPT- 4, which converses more fluently than the previous models. It can also process data faster, understand more text, and even process images. There are rumors about a GPT-5, but that remains to be seen. ChatGPT has a wide variety of uses, from composing emails, advert copies, scripts, cover letters, blogs, and articles to doing more complex stuff like writing programming languages, debugging code, and solving complex problems. It's been used by different people for various uses like writing projects and theses, creating content calendars for social media, writing marketing copies, composing songs, and so on.

Now in the interest of fairness, it's not exactly 100% perfect because it's been implicated in several cases of plagiarism and misinformation (Stringer, 2023). It's also been caught accusing people of false crimes and being toxic when assuming a certain personality. The fact is that there are a few kinks to work out, but that shouldn't stop you from starting your ChatGPT-based side hustle.

Potentials and Limitations of ChatGPT

I asked ChatGPT if there were limitations to how much it could get done, and interestingly, it told me quite a few useful things about what it couldn't do. We'll look at this in a bit.

As much as I appreciate the ease AI brings into our world, it'll be unfair to disregard its limitations because that could play a big role in whatever outcome you get. One big factor to keep in mind is that new updates are frequently made to this particular AI, so whatever we describe as a drawback in this section may very well be possible in the nearest future. When I say that the possibilities are endless, this is what I mean. This is also why you can't afford to stay stale in the industry or cling to old information. Thankfully, this book teaches you what to do and where to go to get the latest scoop on the industry.

I should inform you that apart from considering the potential applications of ChatGPT as an AI operating singly, you'll also need to be open to the possibility of collaborating with other AI that isn't necessarily chatbots to maximize your outcomes.

That being said, let's look at all the fun things you can do with ChatGPT to make money:

1. Write social media posts/ad copies

We all know social media as a place where we go to catch up with people, learn new things and showcase ourselves. You may also be aware that social media is also a great place to make money and thanks to ChatGPT, you'll be able to leverage the power of social media to make more money. It can be used to write engaging, relevant, and compelling posts that are brand aligned and provoke a response from the audience. In time, you'll be able to grow your following, get more likes and shares and even get brand sponsorships and partnerships. You can even use it to translate your content into different languages. You can also get well-detailed email campaigns written by ChatGPT. All these will boost your marketing efforts and ultimately lead to more sales.

Just imagine this, you've created a digital product that costs $50 and you have a following of 600k people. If sixty thousand of those people bought your product at $50, you'd make a whopping $3 million. This is not a drill, it's entirely achievable!

2. Write content for online courses, eBooks, and tutorials

Courses, tutorials, and eBooks are excellent digital products you can sell to an audience primed to need the information you've got. You can use ChatGPT to create content that's informative and simple to understand. You can create an outline and train it to follow that outline. All you'll have to do is review and fine-tune, which takes significantly less time than if you had to write from scratch.

3. Write scripts for video content

One of the limitations ChatGPT has is that it's an entirely text-based platform, so it cannot generate videos/pictures and sound. But there's a workaround for enterprising people like you and me. You can use ChatGPT to create the scripts for your promotional videos or podcasts so that you'll be able to get great results. This means you'll get good audience feedback and more conversions.

We've seen that ChatGPT is the tool to look out for when it comes to creating almost any type of written content. Other potential uses are:

- It can manipulate and process large amounts of data.

- It can answer questions and follow up with further useful information.

- It can take tests. It once took the SATs and scored 52%, which is pretty impressive (Anaconda, 2023).

- It can teach concepts and make them simpler to understand.

- It can write code as well as debug it.

- It can create songs and even write really great poems.

- It can work in 73 different languages.

- It can learn from its experience and interaction with you.

- It can write in a particular style or imitate a particular author if asked.

We already talked about ChatGPT being limited to text-based interactions, which prevents it from doing a lot of stuff. Other important restrictions with ChatGPT use are:

1. It can't access the internet

The ChatGPT interface was trained with a lot of data to give it context and background to generate accurate responses. As great as this has proven to be, the fact that it cannot access the internet means it doesn't have access to updated information and can't crosscheck the information it already has against multiple sources.

Yep, you guessed right, this means that it could provide outdated information and even plagiarize the content it's giving you. Not so great for authenticity.

2. It's a machine

Chatting with ChatGPT can make you feel like you're talking to a super polite assistant who's competent, knowledgeable, and dedicated to helping you. As cool as this may seem, it's still a machine that hasn't mastered the nuances of emotions in human communication. You bet that this means it won't be able to interpret the emotional undertones or add emotional context to the information it's putting out. This means you have to do a thorough job of checking and cross-checking for this as you go along, meaning it may sound stilted and overly formal when you chat with it.

Apart from these two major limitations, some other important drawbacks of the ChatGPT AI technology are :

- It can only take in limited input. It can't analyze a long text or a novel.

- It doesn't give detailed information about topics.

- It can only answer one query at a time and won't move on to the next one until it's done.

- It may not be sustainable in the long run because it's very expensive to maintain.

In case you're wondering, when I asked ChatGPT about its limitations, it told me that:

- It may provide wrong or irrelevant answers because of its limited data pool.

- It doesn't have a body, so it can't give sensory information or do any physical tasks.

- It doesn't have emotions, so it can't relate.

- It needs to be prompted before it responds.

It's pretty spot on, isn't it? Now that you have a clear view of what you can achieve with AI let's talk about what you'll need to do before you start using ChatGPT.

Registering and Setting Up Your ChatGPT

Believe it or not, people lived through the times when they had to either buy a CD or get it delivered to them, all so they could access software or an update. If you're not sure of what a CD is, please look it up. I promise you'll be entertained.

What if I told you that to get access to this money-making AI, you'd have to go all the way to Silicon Valley, find the shallowest river there and try to mine for a precious stone that'll be used to create the right code to get you in? Would you still be as determined as you were when you read the introduction to this book? Probably not. Or maybe you'd see this as yet another challenge and crush it.

Thankfully, you don't have to do anything half as extreme as that to get your hands on the ChatGPT interface. You can use it on your phone and laptop. Here's how to register and set up your own ChatGPT account.

To get started, you'll need:

- Your phone or a laptop

- An active email address

- A strong connection to the internet

1. Start by heading to the OpenAi site

ChatGPT was created by OpenAi, and that's where you'll find it. The first thing to do is create an account on chat.openai.com. When you head to the site, you may not get immediate access or see a message that says, "ChatGPT is at capacity right now." This just shows that many people are on the server, and you need to wait a while.

2. Create your free account

When you get access to the site, you'll see a signup button, which you should click on. You'll need to enter your email address or your Microsoft account details. Then you'll create a strong password that should be at least eight characters long and click on 'continue. '

3. Verify your email address and get started

You'll get an email address with a verification link, which when clicked, takes you to a page where they'll request your name and phone number. Once you type in those details, a verification code will be sent to your phone. You'll need to enter the code sent and then click continue. Voila! You're in! You'll see a page that clearly illustrates ChatGPT's capabilities and limitations with some great examples. You'll also see a text box where you can type in your query. You're good to go!

If you'd like to upgrade to ChatGPT Plus for $20 a month, simply select 'Upgrade to Plus' from the menu on the left side of your screen. You'll have to fill in your payment information and click subscribe at the bottom.

You can now start using your ChatGPT Plus! Try asking questions. Just play around with it and get familiar.

Understanding the ChatGPT Interface

One thing that many ChatGPT users may miss in their excitement to use the chatbot is that its knowledge isn't current. It's only aware of stuff that happened right up to 2021.

Anything after that, and it'll most likely give you inaccurate information.

Just to test this out, I asked ChatGPT who won the 2022 Super Bowl. Its reply was something along the lines of the fact that it didn't have access to information from the future because the 2022 Super Bowl hadn't yet taken place. Now, if you needed to write an ad copy relevant to the Super Bowl with ChatGPT's help, you may get outdated information, which would do your content more harm than good.

If you're wondering why I'm taking the time to talk about this, it's because I know that you're tempted to skip this section as you probably think you know all there is to know about ChatGPT. As tempting as that may be, I'd like to ask you to take the time to read this section. You never know what piece of information you may learn that'll make all the difference. I'll try very hard not to make it boring too. Shall we?

Remember that chapter about the history of AI? We talked about Natural Language Processing, Machine Learning, and Natural Language Understanding. Let's do a little refresh.

Natural Language Processing is the part of AI that deals with helping computers understand how we write and speak. Normally AI interprets information fed to it as neatly batched and structured data. The way we speak and write isn't as structured as the data that the AI is used to, so it's quite a task. That's where NLP comes in. Natural Language Understanding also helps AI understand the nuances and context of our speech. That's why if you tell ChatGPT, "Top of the morning to you," it'll understand that you're saying good morning and reply in kind instead of trying to analyze the earliest part of the morning. Still with me?

Machine learning is another part of AI that lets the algorithm process data without giving it specific instructions or programming. This allows them to learn from their errors, just like we do.

ChatGPT is a Language Learning Model (LLM) device. It was trained with large amounts of data and uses machine learning to generate situationally accurate responses to commands or prompt inputs. So, ChatGPT was allowed to access a very wide range of data from the internet, books, magazines, and so on. With this background, it can simulate human conversation and understand references and some slang. That's why it's so popular –it can mimic human conversation so well that you may be hard-pressed to forget that you're not chatting with a person.

Another important distinction you need to make is that ChatGPT isn't a search engine like Google or Bing because you would be leaving a lot of money on the table if you were to treat it like one. The major difference here is that search engines simply generate web pages with content related to your query. On the other hand, ChatGPT can learn the patterns and statistical relationships your query has to the data in its database. So it's able to provide more information and do a wider variety of tasks.

As an LLM, ChatGPT is trained to understand human interactions, but it doesn't just stop there; it learns how the relationship between words works and uses that knowledge to predict the next words that fit the situation. It receives information in tokens, which are numerical representatives of the words you type into the chatbox. So whenever you ask a question or give a command, the words get broken down into tokens that are processed and compared to the data already available. An appropriate response is generated, which is screened and modified and then presented to you (Ruby, 2022).

The complex interplay of several components of AI ensures that your interactions with ChatGPT are productive. The icing on the cake is that it can learn from its interactions with you, thanks to machine learning, so you can expect better results every time.

ChatGPT Use Cases

I once asked ChatGPT to tell me a funny joke, and it replied:

"Why did the tomato turn red?... Because it saw the salad dressing!"

Well, while we're certainly not hiring it to write a stand-up comedy script soon, there are other marvelous ways you can use it. Let's take a closer look at all the unconventional ways ChatGPT can help you, and you just may be surprised:

1. It can help you sort out your issues

This AI doesn't exactly qualify as a therapist, and I'm not recommending that you skip speaking to a therapist because of ChatGPT, but it can help you with some personal problems. One significant drawback is that it doesn't understand emotions or have feelings, but notwithstanding, it can give you great advice and practical tips to help get you out of a tight spot. Since it's a conversational chatbot, you'll find that it may feel like you're talking to a friend, albeit a very formal one. Of course, it's much better to talk to someone but try it! You never know.

2. It can help prepare you for an interview

If you're trying to get a job and you're interviewing at different places, ChatGPT is the perfect companion for you. Thanks to the data it was trained with, it's quite experienced in several industries and can help you create mock interview questions and probable scenarios that are relevant to you. It'll also offer solutions.

3. It can help you prepare and pass your exams

Just like for job interviews, ChatGPT can draft exam questions and answers for different courses. I don't need to talk about how helpful this can be if you're studying for major exams.

4. It can write jokes

While it's not the wittiest AI ever, ChatGPT can write original jokes that may help you break the ice at social events or when meeting new people. Plus, you can ask it to modify the jokes to your taste.

5. It can help you translate stuff into different languages

If you're marketing a product that you want to sell worldwide, wouldn't you want to be able to communicate with your audience in their languages? Thanks to ChatGPT, you don't have to pay for an expensive translator and can be sure it'll do a great job.

6. It can help you organize games night

You don't have to limit ChatGPT to your business life alone. When you're taking a breather from working on your side hustle, you can just have a fantastic game night with ChatGPT. It can generate riddles, play two truths and a lie and even solve crossword puzzles.

7. It can be a great search engine

Even though its knowledge is limited to events before 2021, ChatGPT can still give original answers and responses to queries. Always be sure to cross-check the sources to avoid plagiarism and the occasional untrue information.

8. It can summarize long texts

Instead of slogging through yet another report, you can ask ChatGPT to summarize the text or site. That way, you get the important facts and can move fast. This saves you a lot of time and potentially helps you make more money.

9. It can help you start a business

ChatGPT is an excellent conversational chatbot that can help you think up business ideas, brainstorm business names, and even suggest how to market them.

If you already have a business idea, it can help you refine your ideas and do some market research to validate your idea or even get a better one.

10. It can be used in the healthcare industry

One way it can be utilized is by responding to patient queries, counseling patients with the right information, or even suggesting ideas for new medicines.

11. It can help you create content and market your business.

Creating emails, blog articles, scriptwriting and ad copies are well within ChatGPT's purview. It can also create personalized content for your customers based on their history. It can consider their past behavior, their demographics, and their demonstrated preferences. It can also help you research your audience so you'll know what they're doing and what they need. It's a superstar with customer support, can conduct keyword research for you, and also write product descriptions.

I hope you'll agree that ChatGPT has a lot of potential and can be used for many aspects of your life. I won't be surprised to see a new wave of start-ups that crop up to solve human problems with AI. Who knows, yours could be next.

Basic Prompts for ChatGPT

I remember attending a house party a few years ago, and I made a new friend. We connected, and it seemed like we were plugged into the same wavelength. We both loved the idea of side hustles, retiring early, and making money work for us. We were both surprised that we'd never met before because we had some friends in common.

Anyway, we exchanged numbers at the end of the night, and

I promised to keep in touch. Unfortunately, I didn't save her number, so I couldn't reach her. I needed to stay in touch with her because we'd exchanged some pretty dope ideas to collaborate and make more money, so what did I do? I reached out to one of our mutual friends, and in no time, I'd gotten her number and re-established contact. That mutual friend was the key to achieving what I needed. That's how important prompt writing is. It's the key to getting the most out of ChatGPT. Your results are only as good as your prompts.

What's a prompt? Whatever you type into the chat box on the ChatGPT user interface. If you type, 'Write a poem,' that's a prompt. If you type, 'Write a poem about love lost and found again,' you'd get more specific results and dare I say, a much better poem than if you'd used the first prompt. That goes to show that there are good and bad prompts.

There are so many prompts for ChatGPT floating around on the Internet, and many of them are really good too. But you'll need to ask ChatGPT to do various things for you, and you can't always rely on the Internet to have the perfect prompt for your situation. We're going to look at the fine art of getting the best results from ChatGPT using the right prompts. Fun fact, there's a hot new tech career, prompt engineering, which is basically about writing the right questions for AI Chatbots like ChatGPT to test their responses and improve their answers. You'll only need basic programming skills and an intimate understanding of prompt writing for chatbots, and you'll be able to make up to $375,000 a year (Business Insider).

Here are some specific guidelines you can use to create better prompts:

1. Define your goal, the channel of communication, and your target audience

This is especially important when you need ChatGPT to do some creative writing for you. If you're tired of getting generic, run-of-the-mill responses, then you need to add as many details as possible.

For example, if you'd like to create content for your podcast, your YouTube video, or an Instagram Reel, instead of typing:

"5 reasons why you need to order product X," try asking ChatGPT to:

"Write a podcast/YouTube /Instagram Reel script for a Gen Z audience who wants to keep fit. Let the script describe how important product X is to achieving their fitness goals. "

From my prompt, you can already see how you'll get a better response than if you'd used the first one.

2. Ask ChatGPT to assume a role

Asking questions without assigning a role may give you good

enough answers, but ask ChatGPT to pretend that it's performing a particular role while answering a query while giving a more appropriate response with better context.

For instance, instead of asking ChatGPT to write an advert copy to sell weight-loss pills, you can write:

"I want you to take on the role of a woman who lost 10 pounds with these weight-loss pills. You're talking weight loss to a group of demotivated, overweight women tired of trying and failing to lose weight. Can you explain why they'd benefit from using the same pills you did? "

I encourage you to try out these two prompts and see the difference yourself.

3.   Break down your results

If you'd like ChatGPT to write a whole page for your website, you're better off asking it to write each step of the content one by one. For example, you can ask it to write the heading first, then ask it to generate subheadings, and then finally flesh out each subheading and the conclusion, one by one.

This method also helps you get around any text limitation that may be present so that your results won't be cut short.

4.   Ask ChatGPT to generate its prompts

This is almost too good to be true, but it works. If you're not sure how to come up with the right prompts for what you need, simply ask ChatGPT to guide you by asking you the right questions you'd need to create the prompts.

With some refinement and further questions, you'll be well on your way to creating the perfect prompts!

Here are some other guidelines to help with creating the perfect prompt:

- Be as specific as possible.

- Use keywords relevant to your topic

- Provide feedback to every response you get, telling ChatGPT exactly how to modify the response for the best results.

- Be as natural as possible when asking questions, and provide as much context as possible.

- Provide examples for ChatGPT to work with. You can show it what you want to achieve and ask it to do something similar.

The essential ingredient needed is patience and a willingness to learn and unlearn. In no time, you'll be writing prompts like a pro!

Integrating your Chat Bot with Other Services

We waxed poetic about all the benefits of ChatGPT and how helpful it is for running our businesses and even our lives. But, if you want to take things a step further, you'll need to merge ChatGPT with your business applications and other relevant services you either use now or will be using in the future to run your business. That's the only way you can use ChatGPT to do all the important business stuff we already discussed.

That's what it means to 'integrate' your ChatGPT chatbot with anything. When you connect it with other apps, it can do more things through those apps like order food, schedule appointments, chat with customers, and so much more. I don't mean to imply that you're late to the party, but a lot of businesses have already integrated chatbots like ChatGPT into their service applications with awesome results. You already know about its advanced NLP capabilities that allow users to get that human feel when interacting with it. I hope you've tried out ChatGPT for yourself and even played around with some of the prompts by now.

Imagine this. You're working a 9 to 5 somewhere with an hour commute both ways. You're home by 6 pm, so you grab a quick, healthy dinner and take a shower then settle in front of your laptop for two hours of focused work. You check your emails and see that 15 new people have signed up for your email list, and 10 of them have bought your course, which you're selling for $49.99. You briefly wonder if they got welcome emails and the course support when they paid for your program. You double-check to confirm that emails have been sent, and indeed they have. You quickly hop onto Instagram and LinkedIn to answer the few comments that ChatGPT didn't respond to.

Then you modify next week's content sequence slightly because you had a great idea you wanted to try out at work, take a calming cup of chamomile tea and prepare for bed at 10 pm, happy that you've made almost $500 today without doing anything active. All thanks to ChatGPT. You can write copies for ads, set up a funnel, move your leads to your email list, welcome them, and set them up on the course platform with the aid of ChatGPT. You fall asleep, dreaming of soft, white, fluffy clouds and happiness.

That's how a typical day running your side hustle with ChatGPT should and will look like once you've successfully integrated your website and other applications you use to it. You can integrate ChatGPT to different websites and apps, but this feature is only available on ChatGPT Plus, which costs a $20 monthly subscription. OpenAi has an API, which means Application Programme Interface, a set of rules or instructions that determine how an app communicates with other third-party tools or apps. ChatGPT has its API, which is only available on the paid version but billed separately. You can easily integrate ChatGPT with any app or website via its API; simply subscribe to an API key on the paid GPT4 version. You'll need a developer or someone with some technical expertise to guide you.

You can use a chatbot builder platform to integrate ChatGPT into your website if you need a more comprehensive option. If you want more options and can dedicate the technical resources to it, you can do a custom implementation, which consists of building your own chatbot and integrating it with an API. This process is super complex, and you'd need to hire experienced and competent developers to do this, but it offers a lot of flexibility.

For the most part, integrating with the API should be good enough for you, although this largely depends on how complex your operations will be. Either way, it'll be fun, plus you'll make a lot of cool cash. Not too shabby, huh?

PART TWO

When last did you go on a roller coaster ride? I don't know about you, but the pretty wild ones lull you into thinking that maybe the ride just isn't that edgy at first before looping or twisting in some hair-raising turns that are sure to see you screaming your heart out. Exhilarating times.

In the first part of this book, you learned everything you needed to know about ChatGPT and AI in general. That's a very important introduction because we're going to be working with AI a lot. Of course, you had to learn a lot of technical terms and maybe know a bit more about the technology than you probably wanted to in the first place. So it may have been a little slow or boring. That's the part of the roller coaster ride that has you thinking that you could take a little nap in the middle of it because of how gentle it seems.

Now it's time for the switch. We're going to be looking at all the practical aspects that'll help you start and run your side hustle. Is passive income passive? How much can you really make? How soon can you start, and when can you expect to cash out your first big check? We'll explore all these burning questions and more. You'll learn about the traditional means of making passive income like real estate investing as well as the newer methods like crypto and blockchain.

Why do many new businesses fail? Hint: it has to do with selling to a market that doesn't need their products. Your passive income needs to succeed and be properly set up because it may soon become your full-time source of income when the money starts flowing in. That's why I'll teach you how to pick the right business, choose the right idea, the right platform, the right audience, and even the right product. This isn't fluff; these are the actual steps you'll need to follow to build a successful side hustle. I'm a bit fond of dwelling on very important facts, and that's why you'll see me repeat some principles throughout this book because some facts simply cannot be overemphasized. The first is that a passive income doesn't start by being all chill and easy like a Sunday morning. Nope. You'll have to put in the work, set it up and guide it so it can work without needing much of your attention, just like a baby. If you jumped into this book expecting to learn how to set up two-hour work weeks side hustles right off the bat, then you have some rethinking to do.

However, I guarantee that you'll enjoy the perks of all the work you put in and finally escape to the tropical paradise you've always dreamed of. You'll learn practical things like how to build websites and create high-quality content that converts your audience to customers. You'll find out the best way to do this with the help of your trusty AI assistants. You'll see how to avoid the common AI pitfalls that rookies unwittingly stumble into and how to always stay updated on the AI industry. Innovation is the name of the game, and you'll be the MVP by the time you're done with this part.

Chapter Three

Ai-Powered Passive Income

"If you don't find a way to make money while you sleep, you will work until the day you die."
– Warren Buffett

If you were to take a short stroll on the internet, you'll most likely be bombarded with books, courses, tutorials, and even nano degrees that promise to teach you how to make a fantastic amount of money every month by simply playing on your laptop for two hours a month and lying around on the beach for the remaining amount of time. I'm not trying to knock any of those products, but I'm sure you've most likely bought one or two of those things and seen that they really didn't have anything to offer. Trust me; I've been there. On the other hand, there have been some really valuable resources that I've learned from and that have contributed to my skill and experience so far. The principles of creating multiple streams of passive income work.

The true beauty of this book is that we're introducing a catalyst to these basic principles - AI. That's your smoking gun right there. All of this is to say you need to know how passive income works and the rules guiding it. Then you need to see how to introduce AI into the mix to make the work faster and free up your time. Is it possible to use this free time to create even more AI-powered streams of passive income? Am I giving you any ideas yet?

Definition and Types of Passive Income

Here's a well-kept secret that most wealthy people don't want you to know: you can make much more money by doing less work. You wouldn't believe how common this practice is; millions of people engage in it daily. That's what passive income is, in a nutshell. It's the money you earn with little to no effort, and it always sets you on the path to financial freedom quicker than other means of making money.

In the technical sense of the word, it means the money you get from a business where you're not actively engaged. Earning money with little to no additional work over months or years is possible through passive income. The beauty of it is that you don't have to trade your time for money as you would at a typical 9 to 5 job. Instead, you do things like owning a building or purchasing an asset that can bring in money, whether at your desk or on the slopes.

Although the prospect of getting paid without effort may sound appealing, there is a catch. You need to put in the time and effort upfront to create the product you'll be selling, whether it's a book, a course, or some other type of asset. You often have to do this without immediate compensation in the expectation of future gain.

The perks of this type of income revolve mainly around the fact you don't need to show up every day to be productive. Your earnings aren't determined by the number of hours in a day you work, your health, your age, the pay scale at your workplace, or your manager's opinion of your performance. You can make more money even if you don't put in a lot of time. You also get more free time to do other things once your passive income source starts paying major bucks. You can afford to retire whenever you want to.

You can earn passive income by:

- Purchasing a cash-producing asset,

- Developing one,

- Investing in one

To generate passive income, you can invest in equities that pay dividends, bonds, annuities, and rental properties. You can buy assets that help you make money, like a vending machine or even a small company. You can also create something that others will pay for, like a course or a book.

One question I get all the time is if the IRS taxes passive income. The answer is yes, although some different terms and conditions apply to each passive income type. You may want to see a tax expert for advice on minimizing your tax liability so you can make the most of your individual situation.

Passive Income Ideas that Work

We've already established that you must invest a lot into a passive income stream first. This may require time, a large chunk of your money, or even both. The key to choosing a passive stream of income that works lies in carefully considering your situation and choosing what works for you. Do you have enough cash to start investing? Do you own an asset or a property you can rent to make more money? Would you prefer to create a business and leverage your time since you don't have a lot of spare cash floating around? Once you can answer these questions, then you're good to go.

Let's take a look at the different strategies for passive income that work:

1. Investing

When you invest, you put your current funds to work to generate additional earnings. You can do this by investing in paid-dividend shares, where you get rewarded with periodic distributions of the company's earnings. The catch here is that you'll need to commit thousands or hundreds of thousands of dollars to get a substantial income from dividend stocks. One major drawback of this method is that some companies may experience financial difficulties and be unable to pay dividends.

You can also invest in real estate by buying a property to resell or rent. One nifty way to invest in real estate without buying whole properties is through Real Estate Investment Trusts(REITs). They help you manage your investments and see that your dividends are paid. Another option is joining crowdfunding platforms to invest in a property and share profits afterward.

2. Renting out assets

If you already own a house, a spare room, a piece of land, or a timeshare condo, you can make money by putting up these assets for rent. All you'll need to do is take a few hours per week to maintain the property and relate with your tenants.

One overlooked asset that you can get into is a vending machine. Sure, you'll have to splurge with a couple of thousand dollars to buy it and set it up, but if it's placed in a busy location, you may find yourself making your money back sooner than later. You can even outsource its servicing and restocking if you're pressed for time.

You have to be creative here and study the market. Do you have a car but don't need it because you'd rather commute to work than bother paying for parking? Great. Rent out your car to someone interested in being a Lyft or Uber driver. Easy peasy.

This method may not be practical for you if you don't have the cash or the asset already. In that case, you'll want to look at the next point.

3.   Creating an asset from scratch

This is the best option if you have little or no capital to start. The main idea is to create something people can willingly exchange their money for. This means that whatever you're offering must meet their needs. There are so many ways to do this, and the idea you choose depends on various factors like your location, your interests, market needs and so on.

One of the most common ways to do this is called dropshipping. All you need to do is find a supplier that sells a particular product at wholesale prices, find a market hungry for that product, add a little profit to the price of each item, and sell to the audience. Once they place their order, the wholesaler fulfills it, and you get to keep the cash on top. Sweet right?

You can also do stuff like creating an eBook full of valuable information to sell or create blog posts with affiliate links so that you'll make some money whenever anyone purchases the product you refer them to. You can also:

- Create online courses

- Create tutorials or worksheets

- Put together a print-on-demand company

- Become a content creator and Influencer online

- Start a YouTube channel

and so much more. Are you getting the hang of this already?

Examples of AI-Powered Passive Income Businesses

Thanks to how useful AI can be, we've found that creating passive streams of income can take on a different outlook than you could imagine. You can use AI to carry out any of the three major means of growing a passive income. Isn't that amazing? So you can either invest, buy, or create a passive source of income with AI.

Let's see how to achieve that:

1. Content creation

I'm sure you've heard many people say that content is king, and I have to agree. Creating content goes beyond recording videos and social media posts. Those are great, too, but you don't have to do all that. You can simply use AI to create content centered around a topic you're interested in, and they could be articles or blog posts packed full of informative and valuable facts. Then add affiliate links to products related to what you're selling and get paid when people purchase these products through your link. Simple.

2. Build your own chatbots

Chatbots and AI helpers like ChatGPT are invaluable, and who says you can't get a slice of that pie? You can choose to create your chatbot with ChatGPT's help or outsource it to a freelancer on a legit freelance site.

Of course, before you do this, you'll need to first check for businesses or organizations that need your service. You could take things a step further and pitch your services to them, especially if you've seen a need for a chatbot. You don't have to look too far; you could start with your favorite app or program. This will always be a crowd-pleaser because almost everyone will benefit from an AI helper to save money and make their processes easier. Once you have one, you can pitch to other companies and get more clients.

3. AI-Powered stock market investing

AI platforms now help you make data-driven investment decisions that are most likely to yield maximum profit. AI studies thousands of stocks and can predict the best options to grow your money. The best part is that you can program the AI tool to make certain decisions in the event of certain occurrences, so you don't have to keep popping back in to check on your investment.

4. Sell AI-generated Art

Thanks to the pandemic, many people are now beautifying their spaces and homes to be as welcoming and aesthetically pleasing. One major way they achieve this is by hanging beautiful wall art in their homes and offices. Generate some beautiful art with Midjourney or Jasper Art, both AI platforms, and sell them online. You can connect it to a third-party printing company that can print on demand and make cool cash without doing anything.

5. Create a course or tutorial with AI

If you're into information marketing with little cash to spare, you can create and upload an entire course or tutorial with, you guessed it, AI. ChatGPT is a good one to help you research and curate the content. This will be initially time-consuming as you create the course, set up a marketing campaign and funnel to advertise and generate leads, but once all that is set up, all you have to do is sit down and watch your cash roll in, for the most part.

6. Sell Data

You can use AI-based techniques and applications to enhance and perfect many parts of the online shopping process for both retailers and consumers. Artificial intelligence (AI) can examine a customer's habits and choices to tailor future interactions to them. Individualized product recommendations, targeted advertising efforts, and one-of-a-kind online content are all instances of this type of personalization. It could also take into account a user's actions, preferences, and past purchases to provide recommendations. Selling this service to small and medium business owners is a great way to make extra income. You can also gather as much information as possible with the help of AI models and then sell to businesses that can use it. Businesses and academic institutions continually seek new information that may help them better serve their customers, increase their competitiveness, and reduce their losses.

These are all easy ways to start making money on the side with AI, and I'm sure you've already spotted one or two possibilities you can get into. What's holding you back again?

Real Estate Investing

AI plus real estate is a combination that can make anyone a lot of profit. Let me ask, how would you rate the relative value of various housing choices? The common practice in the real estate sector is for people to weigh available data and use their intuition when making important choices. This traditional approach is good because you get to monitor current market conditions and past track records.

On average, the old-fashioned real estate investor gets to make a tidy amount of profit with this method, and once you add AI to the mix, the possibilities are endless. As businesses in the commercial real estate industry gain access to more market data, they can use machine learning and AI to analyze different assets with a set of criteria. This information may be gathered from various sources, including market conditions, business practices, tenant interest, and socioeconomic difficulties. AI can also make quarterly and annual estimates of market and submarket growth and help with underwriting property. You'll get to see how the information available, like lease transaction data, average unoccupied days, retention rates, lease lengths, and other operational estimates, can help make better decisions.

In addition, AI software can analyze data for trends and predict future events. Imagine being able to predict the neighbor's behaviors, understand tenants' routines, and foresee the need for repairs. Wouldn't you be the most efficient landlord or property manager on the planet? Also, this information can show you if it's a good idea to invest in a particular property, especially if it'll cost too much to manage.

If you're renting out a property for Airbnb, AI can help you save unnecessary utility bills by turning off lights, the thermostat, and other equipment between tenants. Installing motion detector lights is a good form of security and may even be a point that makes your tenants feel safe and secure throughout their stay. You'll be able to track when their tenants enter and exit the building. You can maximize efficiency by linking your tenant's normal heating and waking-up routines. That way, you're enhancing their quality of life, lowering costs, and saving the environment simultaneously! All thanks to AI. Not all heroes wear capes.

If you're looking to get into the real estate investment industry by renting out properties to long-term tenants, using Airbnb, or even renting out commercial properties, here are some apps you need to know about:

1. Zillow 3D Home

This AI-powered platform allows real estate agents to create photorealistic 3D virtual tours of available properties. You can make a 3D model of the property and send it to interested tenants so they can do a virtual walkthrough before making an offer. This means you don't have to be available to show your property to various potential tenants, saving you time and money.

2. RealtyMogul

This is an automated property search and investment tool that uses machine learning algorithms to analyze property data and give recommendations to investors and brokers. If you're not looking to manage property directly, you can use this tool to get great investment recommendations.

3. Matterport

This service allows users to create lifelike 3D and virtual reality tours of properties. You can use it to create 3D interactive models of your property on the market.

4. Roof Ai

This AI-powered program estimates the financial requirements of roofing jobs. Machine learning algorithms are applied to data about properties to provide estimates for roofing projects.

5. RealCrowd

This is another AI tool you can use to locate and analyze profitable real estate deals. Using machine learning algorithms, it analyzes property data and provides recommendations to investors and brokers.

6. Homie

If you're looking for a virtual real estate agent powered by AI, Homie is your best bet! This application uses Machine Learning and Natural Language Processing to carry on natural dialogues with users, answering their questions and easing their fears about the home-buying process.

7. Haus

This is an AI-powered real estate search and home-buying platform. Using machine learning algorithms, it analyzes property data and provides recommendations to investors and brokers.

The idea is to apply AI to as many real estate investment processes as possible to get better recommendations, save money and time, and make as much money as possible. You can choose to be as active or passive as you'd like.

Stock Market Investing

Let's be honest, the stock market has a reputation for being volatile, unpredictable, and without a discernible pattern. Factors such as politics, the global economy, unanticipated occurrences, and a company's financial performance make it difficult to forecast stock values. That hasn't stopped people like Warren Buffett from making big bucks off the stock market, but in the same way, many people also lose a lot of money every day, thanks to stock market investing.

Financial decision-makers have relied on stock market forecasting since the late 19th century. Stock prices were predicted using statistical models created in the early 20th century. These models considered corporate profitability, economic statistics, and market patterns. In the early 1900s, Charles Dow developed the Dow Theory. The advent of the personal computer in the 1960s and '70s allowed academics to develop more sophisticated models for predicting stock prices. Now that AI is in the mix, the goal has been to develop new and improved techniques of analysis that may be used to predict future stock market movements.

"AI trading" refers to automating the examination of historical market and stock data, generating investment ideas, constructing investment portfolios, and buying and selling stocks. Using machine learning, sentiment analysis, and complex mathematical projections, AI stock trading sifts through millions of data points to execute profitable bets. The ability of AI traders to properly and effectively evaluate forecast markets can significantly improve risk management and return on investment.

Since research and data-driven decision-making are automated with AI trading, as an investor you'll spend less time on research and more time supervising transactions. Researchers found that merchants who used algorithmic trading were 10% more productive (The Trade, 2022). Artificial intelligence trading utilizes accumulated financial data to enhance efficiency and accuracy. Sentiment analysis combined with AI trading allows for the prediction of patterns while also saving money, working around the clock, and keeping a close check on the stock market. Precision, rapidity, and dependability are just a few advantages of using AI for financial market predictions.

Artificial intelligence (AI) has the potential to greatly improve stock market forecasts by, among other things, the rapid and precise processing of massive data sets. Artificial intelligence may identify data patterns, providing more thorough and reliable results than human analysts could achieve on their own. Because AI can rapidly scan massive databases, this enables real-time insights into market patterns and pricing movements. In addition, AI can provide individualized guidance to help owners prepare for and respond to possible threats.

These AI trading firms use a wide range of AI capabilities, like the analysis of market data, the calculation of price changes, the identification of the causes of price variations, the execution of sales and trades, and the constant monitoring of the market. Thanks to AI, traders can carry out quantitative, algorithmic, high-frequency, and automated trading in the financial markets. Algorithmic trading relies on predetermined rules based on past data, while quantitative trading uses quantitative modeling to examine stock prices and trading volumes.

There are different types of AI trading firms you can check out, like Canoe, which specializes in alternative investments, such as venture capital, art and antiques, hedge funds, and commodities, and uses natural language processing, machine learning, and meta-data analysis to verify and categorize an investor's documentation. Another one, AlphaSense, uses AI trading technology like natural language processing and machine learning to comb through thousands of documents, market reports, and press releases.

Whew, that was a mouthful.

Of course, if you're so inclined, you can create your AI trading bot, but you'd need to have the relevant data as well as some expertise on the investment scene. If not, you can comfortably invest in credible AI trading firms and let your money work for you. The bottom line is that stock market investing together with AI and its ability to process data and calculate variables is a marriage made to last and you should take advantage of it.

Blockchain and Cryptocurrency

There are two kinds of people in the world. Those that are fully on the crypto /blockchain train and can hold rousing debates on issues related to this topic. Then we have those that immediately zone out when they hear the term 'blockchain' and have perhaps only encountered crypto when they tried to pay for something or get paid. It doesn't matter which of the classes you belong to; you need to know how to make money from AI concerning these two. Not to worry, we'll talk plainly and keep things as simple as possible.

I figure we can start by asking what blockchain means and why it's so important. In the simplest of terms, a blockchain is a technology that ensures that whatever information is recorded with it cannot be easily altered, hacked, or used fraudulently. A blockchain comprises computer systems connected within it, serving as a digital account book of transactions that are transparently duplicated and shared with all the computers on the blockchain. So this means that every time a new transaction takes place, it is recorded and added to each member of the blockchain. Instead of having one centralized database, it operates in a decentralized database accessed and managed by multiple members. The special thing about blockchains is that each transaction in that ecosystem is recorded with a unique cryptographic marking called a hash. The advantage of working in a blockchain is that any attempt to change the data would be immediately apparent to everyone in the ecosystem because it affects them all. There's also a level of security because all the records in the blockchain are encrypted.

That's what a blockchain is; this technology is starting to gain ground and is being integrated into various types of platforms and hardware all over the world. There are different types of blockchains; we have public blockchains that are open for communal participation and use a token; private blockchains are smaller and closely controlled blockchains that do not use a token; and we have permissioned blockchains that limit individual action in their system.

Cryptocurrency is a term that almost always comes up whenever blockchain is being discussed. If you're wondering why, it's because cryptocurrency cannot exist without blockchain in the first place. Have you ever tried to make any kind of sandwich without bread? Useless, I know, because bread is the foundation of all sandwiches, no matter how fancy you make it sound. Blockchain is the system that allows for cryptocurrency to exist in the first place; it's like the foundation. A cryptocurrency is like digital money; it transfers value from one person to another. Bitcoin is a type of cryptocurrency that operates as a blockchain and is the biggest so far. People can trust this form of currency because it's decentralized and secure, thanks to the blockchain technology it's based on. As we've established, there are different cryptocurrencies, but bitcoin seems to be the most secure.

Now to the most important part of this section-how to make money from crypto with AI. Here are some easy ways:

1. Create content

Yep, there's content again, always turning up like a, in this case, good coin. A lot of people still don't know what Crypto is about and how to maximize it. That's where you come in with wonderfully informative AI-generated content that informs, educates, and enriches your audience. You don't have to do much, but you do have to be consistent. Set up a website or a blog to publish content. Choose one or two social media platforms, create engaging content with AI again, and drive the traffic to your website.

You'll be able to make money from ads and affiliate links. You may even get sponsorship deals from other crypto brands.

2. Crypto investing

You can invest in different cryptocurrencies when their entry price is low and sell them at a higher price. This is the basis of crypto investing. You'll need to be able to predict the highs and lows of the market to know when to buy and when to hold. With AI, you'll be able to predict the market trends and make informed decisions to make you the most profit without having to stay glued to your screen the entire time.

3. Crypto trading

Like the stock market, the crypto market needs to be properly researched before making trades. You'll need to buy some cryptocurrency and trade it for others to make money. This is riskier than any other kind of investing because the crypto market is notoriously volatile. With AI, you can study market trends and make accurate predictions. You can set your trader bot to hold and sell at predetermined conditions, so you won't get to lose much. You can also create a community of crypto investors and give them access to your signals for a price.

4. Invest in AI related projects

Every day, a new company comes up to create some AI solution that's sure to be needed and useful. Most of these companies ask for investors to get in on the action early. You can invest in projects like this and make your money back and profit. Be sure to do your research before investing so you don't get scammed.

You can determine the extent of your involvement on the

crypto scene, but I'd encourage you to try as many streams of income as possible till you find the one that works for you. Of course, you'll need to research and dedicate time to take consistent action, but you'll eventually strike gold, trust me.

Chapter Four

Getting Started

"When your money makes more than you do, you are officially wealthy."
– Dave Ramsey

While trying to find something substantial to get you started on this path, I found something interesting about a couple. Their story will interest you.

Shane and Jocelyn Sams were two teachers who worked in a school in southern Kentucky. Back in 2012, they came up with a small online business idea that eventually made them millionaires. But that wasn't how it started.

They got tired of their regular 9 to 5 jobs, which paid around $5,000 per month after taxes, plus they didn't like their boss. They wanted to do something more exciting with their lives.

So, Shane started trying out how to make money with affiliate blogs and started creating websites where he would share different things. At first, he didn't make much money, just a few bucks. Jocelyn noticed what Shane was doing, and together they started thinking of ways to make more money with their online business.

They decided to use their teaching skills and knowledge to their advantage. They began offering lesson plans, e-books, and other teacher resources on their Elementary Librarian website. Their site started growing quickly, and they started making a lot of money. Eventually, they could quit their teaching jobs and focus entirely on their online business.

You see, that's one way to go about it – turning your passion into something that can lead to a better lifestyle and more income. And that would be the take-off point for this chapter.

How do you know what online business to start?

Choosing a Niche

You can learn many things about starting an online business and personal branding, but it can be overwhelming at times. One important piece of advice you'll often hear is to find your "niche," which means focusing on a specific area you're passionate about and want to specialize in.

Having a genuine niche can be really beneficial when starting an online business. When you choose a niche, it means you're focusing on a specific area that you're truly passionate about and have expertise in. This can give you a competitive edge and make your business stand out.

By selecting a niche for your online business, you can cater to a specific target audience. Instead of trying to appeal to everyone, you can tailor your products or services to meet your niche market's unique needs and interests. This helps you connect with your customers on a deeper level, building trust and loyalty.

When you establish yourself as an authority in a particular niche, it becomes easier to gain a following. People who are interested in that niche will be more likely to seek out your content, products, or services because you're offering something they specifically want or need. This can lead to increased visibility, engagement, and ultimately, business success.

Choosing a niche also allows you to focus your efforts and resources more effectively. Instead of spreading yourself too thin by trying multiple businesses, you can concentrate on becoming an expert in your chosen niche. This enables you to provide valuable and specialized content, products, or services that resonate with your target audience.

So, when starting an online business, take the time to carefully choose a niche that aligns with your passions, expertise, and the needs of your target audience. With the right niche and a solid strategy, you'll be on your way to creating a successful and fulfilling online venture.

Here's a guide on how to choose your niche:

➤ **Explore Your Passions**

- Identify what genuinely interests you.

- Consider activities you enjoy during your free time.

- Reflect on subjects you are curious about and love learning.

➤ **Address Customer Needs**

- Find solutions to problems your potential customers face.

- Conduct market research and brainstorm ideas.

- Utilize tools like Google Trends to identify areas of interest and market gaps.

➤ **Target Your Ideal Audience**

- Focus on connecting with individuals who align with your values.

- Seek out customers who share your interests and preferences.

- Building brand loyalty and a successful business relies on attracting the right audience.

➢ Seek Valuable Feedback

- Engage in conversations and gather insights from family, colleagues, and potential customers.

- Network with professionals in similar fields to understand specific needs.

- Utilize feedback to improve your offerings.

➢ Prioritize Long-Term Growth

- Avoid placing excessive financial pressure on yourself initially.

- Building a profitable business takes time and persistence.

- Focus on sustainable growth rather than immediate monetary gains.

➢ Study Competitors

- Analyze competitors to gain valuable insights.

- Take notes on their strategies, branding, and content.

- Ensure your work remains original while learning from others.

> **Highlight Your Unique Selling Point**

- Identify what sets your product or service apart.

- Emphasize your distinctive features or benefits.

- Let your creativity shine in showcasing what makes you unique.

> **Test and Refine**

- Validate your niche by testing it through various methods.

- Create a website, engage in direct outreach, or participate in business fairs.

- Seek exposure to different ideas and continuously improve your own.

> **Regularly Evaluate and Adapt**

- Continuously reassess your business strategy.

- Consider profitability, target audience, and consumer solutions.

- Successful businesses reflect and readjust regularly to stay relevant and grow.

But do you know what?

If you dream of making millions of dollars through your online business and being recognized for your message and problem-solving abilities, you need to think on a grander scale.

According to Lawrence (2021), truly great and influential people don't limit themselves to a specific niche; don't limit yourself to just one, either. However, after you've identified your passion, if you discover you've got multi-passions, start with one – the one that rates high on your passion list and is viable for the market. Focus on that one. You can add others later to form a chain of online businesses.

Identifying your Target Audience

Laja (2019), a renowned conversion optimization champion, once said that if you think your website (or your online business) is for everyone or anyone interested in your services, it's unlikely to help you increase conversions.

NB: *When a visitor to your website accomplishes a specific goal, like filling out a form or making a purchase, it's called a conversion.*

So, to boost conversions, it's essential to identify your main target audience and understand their wants, needs, priorities, and the challenges they face. By doing so, you can address their specific concerns and eliminate any obstacles that may hinder their engagement.

Peter Drucker (cited by Laja, 2019) stated that marketing aims to understand your customer so deeply that your product or service perfectly matches their needs, making it easy to sell without much effort.

One of the critical questions you must ask yourself while trying to identify your target audience is, "Who are the people that need my services?" Don't be under the illusion that everyone does. No! Don't squander your initial zest on people who don't need what you're offering. It's just right to invest time in conducting personal research (Laja, 2019) to identify your target audience and tailor your service to meet their needs. Got that?

Just so you know, your target audience is a specific group of consumers that you want to reach through your marketing efforts to promote and sell your product or service. It represents the people most likely to be interested in and purchase what you offer.

For example, suppose you have a new line of skateboarding shoes. Your target audience could be skateboarders between the ages of 15 and 25, residing in urban areas, who actively engage in skateboarding culture and follow popular skateboarding influencers. They are passionate about skateboarding, value comfort and durability in shoes, and are willing to spend a certain amount on high-quality skateboarding footwear.

The target audience is defined by various characteristics, including:

- Demographics – age, location, gender, income, etc.

- Interests

- Lifestyle choices

These details help you tailor your marketing messages and strategies to reach and connect with your target audience effectively.

Here are simplified steps to help you identify your target audience:

1. Understand Your Customers

- Analyze your current customer base and conduct client interviews.

- Learn about their age, location, and interests.

- Engage with them on social media or through customer surveys.

2. Research Your Market

- Study the market research in your industry.

- Identify service gaps that your product can fill.

- Look at trends in similar products to find your unique value.

3. Study Your Competitors

- Analyze your competitors to see who they are targeting.

- Observe their marketing channels (online or offline).

- Determine if they focus on decision-makers or supporters.

4. Create Target Personas

- Develop personas to understand different segments of your target audience.

- Consider demographics, personalities, and needs.

- Use data, surveys, and digital interactions to shape the personas.

- Aim to create three to five personas for a comprehensive

view.

5. Define Exclusions

- Determine who is not part of your target audience.

- Be specific about your demographic, e.g., women between 20 and 40.

- Avoid spending resources on segments that won't yield returns.

6. Continuously Refine

- Gather more data and interact with customers to improve understanding.

- Optimize and refine your personas based on new insights.

7. Utilize Google Analytics

- Leverage Google Analytics for valuable insights on website users.

- Identify channels where your target audience comes from.

- Analyze their engagement with content to make data-driven decisions in media planning.

Conducting Market Research

Found this interesting narrative on *Bigcommerce*:

In 2011, Ron Johnson, an experienced business executive, took on the role of CEO at JCPenney. Having previously held high-level positions at Target and Apple, he seemed like a promising choice for the company.

With confidence, JCPenney embraced Johnson's decision to revolutionize its business by eliminating coupons, promotions, and sales events. They believed this would lead to growth and success.

However, things didn't go as planned. JCPenney experienced a decline in sales and lost customers. The rebranding effort turned into what Forbes later described as an epic fail.

So, what went wrong? Johnson made a critical mistake—he failed to understand the brand's target audience. In an interview, he admitted that he thought people were tired of coupons and similar promotions. Unfortunately, it turned out that JCPenney customers actually loved those discounts and sales.

Let me reiterate: Don't ever make assumptions about your customers' wants. Never, ever!

Quantitative and qualitative research can better guide your

decision-making process. And by gathering data and insights from various sources, you can better understand your target audience and make informed business decisions.

Whenever you want to conduct your market research, you need to bear in mind that when it comes to online market research, there are generally two main categories to explore: primary and secondary research. Additionally, within these categories, you'll encounter qualitative and quantitative research methods.

Let's break it down further:

1. Primary Market Research

- This involves gathering data directly from your target audience or market.

- Examples of primary research methods include surveys, interviews, focus groups, and observations.

- It helps you gain firsthand insights specific to your business or product.

2. Secondary Market Research

- This involves using existing data and information that others have already collected.

- Secondary research sources can include reports,

industry studies, government data, and published articles.

- It provides a broader perspective on the market, industry trends, and competitor analysis.

3. Qualitative Research

- Qualitative research focuses on understanding people's opinions, experiences, and motivations.

- It involves techniques such as interviews, focus groups, and open-ended surveys.

- Qualitative research provides rich, descriptive insights and allows for deeper exploration of customer attitudes and behaviors.

4. Quantitative Research

- Quantitative research focuses on collecting numerical data and analyzing it statistically.

- This research method involves surveys, experiments, and data analysis tools.

- It provides statistical evidence and allows for generalization and numerical comparisons.

By considering these different approaches, you can tailor your online market research to gather the most relevant and useful information for your business. Remember, a combination of primary and secondary research, along with qualitative and quantitative methods, can provide a well-rounded understanding of your target market and help inform your business decisions.

So, *how should you conduct market research for your online business?*

To answer this, I curated suggestions from Brett Regan, a content marketing manager, and Liz March, a digital research specialist. Below are their suggestions:

Here are different ways to conduct online market research:

1. Define your research objectives

Clearly identify what you want to learn from your research, whether it's finding new market opportunities, exploring potential growth areas, or refining your product ideas.

2. Choose the right research methods

Consider the type of data you need and select the appropriate market research methods. There are four core types to choose from: primary market research, secondary market research, qualitative market research, and quantitative market research.

3. Conduct keyword research

Use tools like Google Keyword Planner, Keyword Tool, or Ahrefs to understand the demand and search volume for specific products or services. Analyze relevant keywords, assess competition, and evaluate business potential based on search results.

4. Analyze the competition

Study your main competitors to gain insights into their business models, sales funnels, and website design. Identify what works, what doesn't, and areas for optimization. Take note of their strengths and weaknesses to inform your own strategies.

5. Research current trends

Utilize Google Trends to understand the interest and seasonality of products or services. Explore upcoming trends from different angles and consider niche opportunities. Be cautious of short-lived fads and focus on sustainable, long-lasting business ideas.

6. Utilize social media

Dive into social media platforms to gather consumer insights. Follow influencers in your industry, monitor relevant hashtags, and analyze competitor sentiment. Consider using text analytics software to extract relevant information from large volumes of online content.

7. Build an online store and test the market

Choose an ecommerce platform that suits your needs and set up your website. Drive traffic to your store through various channels like SEO, content marketing, and social media. Launch your business and gather firsthand feedback from potential customers.

8. Leverage forums and customer feedback

Engage with online niche forums to learn about your target audience's preferences. Contribute to discussions, ask questions, and gain insights. Additionally, gather feedback from your existing customers through online surveys, interviews, and automated feedback emails. Pay attention to unsolicited customer feedback, even if it's negative, as it can provide valuable insights.

Creating Your Digital Products

This is a step further from knowing your target audience and conducting market research. If you don't go through those phases, you won't know the fitting product to create that will meet your audience's needs.

The Internet offers a unique opportunity to start a business with minimal investment and risk. However, it requires proactive steps rather than passive contemplation.

Here's how to start:

Step 1: Create an Engaged Email List with an Autoresponder

Building an email list through an autoresponder is vital for bringing your audience together and informing them about your offerings. Start with a simple autoresponder and craft messages that address their problems, share your mission, and highlight your solution.

Step 2: Engage Your Audience with Compelling Cornerstone Content

Develop cornerstone content that addresses the most important questions in your niche. Focus on frequently asked and the questions you wish people would ask. While it doesn't have to be perfect initially, continuously refine and expand your cornerstone content over time.

Step 3: Expand Your Network for Opportunities and Collaborations

Actively expand your network to maximize opportunities for your new venture. Guest posting on relevant platforms is a great way to reach a broader audience and connect with other professionals. Additionally, leverage social media channels to engage with content publishers and provide value without being overly promotional.

Step 4: Gather Market Insights for Informed Product Creation

Content: Before diving into product creation, deeply understand your target audience's needs and desires. Utilize social media platforms to listen attentively to their challenges, frustrations with existing solutions, and the obstacles holding them back. Consider conducting free Q&A sessions to gather specific questions and provide valuable insights.

Step 5: Develop Your Minimum Viable Product (MVP)

The culmination of your research leads to the development of your Minimum Viable Product (MVP). Identify the smallest product or service that can benefit your audience. It doesn't have to be a paid product initially; consider offering free offerings to test the market. Launch your MVP, gather feedback, and analyze its reception to make necessary improvements and optimizations.

Step 6: Refine and Scale Your Product Based on Feedback

Once you have a product that resonates with your audience, focus on refining and scaling it. Continuously gather feedback, analyze user insights, and make necessary adjustments to enhance the user experience. As you gather more data and insights, scale your product to reach a wider audience and maximize its impact.

Creating a Business Plan

It's great that you've decided to start an online business. I know this because you're still reading this book.

Now, to turn your vision for an online business into a profitable venture, it's crucial to develop a comprehensive e-commerce business plan. This plan will provide you with a roadmap and ensure you have all the necessary elements to make your e-commerce business successful.

Having a business plan for your online store is essential. It not only helps you define your target market and identify your ideal customers but also enables you to establish clear monthly and quarterly sales goals. By setting specific targets, you can track your progress and make adjustments as needed to increase the likelihood of long-term e-commerce success.

A well-crafted business plan also allows you to analyze the competitive landscape, identify potential challenges, and develop strategies to overcome them. It provides a solid foundation for making informed decisions about product selection, pricing, marketing tactics, and operational processes.

Additionally, a business plan can be beneficial if you seek funding or investment for your e-commerce business, as it demonstrates your professionalism and commitment to achieving your goals.

Follow this guide to know what to include in your business plan:

Executive Summary - Summarize Your Business Plan

In the Executive Summary of your business plan, give a brief overview of your business objectives and mission. Share the problems your business aims to solve for your clients and express your motivations and goals. It's usually best to write this section last after you've outlined all the other details.

Example:

The Executive Summary provides a snapshot of our business plan for HealthyBite, an online subscription-based meal delivery service. Our mission is to make healthy eating convenient and accessible for busy individuals by delivering nutritious and delicious meals to their doorstep.

Through our carefully curated menu and personalized meal plans, we aim to address the challenge of maintaining a healthy diet in today's fast-paced lifestyle. Our goal is to establish HealthyBite as a leading player in the meal delivery industry and achieve sustainable growth in the coming years.

Business Description - Share Your Vision

Describe your business from your perspective and discuss your growth plans. Explain the sources of your profits and clarify the types of customers you will target. Highlight how your products or services will specifically help them.

Example:

HealthyBite is a digital platform that offers a wide range of chef-prepared, nutrient-rich meals. Our vision is to revolutionize the way people approach their dietary habits and provide them with a convenient solution for maintaining a healthy lifestyle.

We will generate revenue through subscription plans and additional revenue streams such as offering specialized dietary options and partnering with local gyms and wellness centers. Our target customers include health-conscious individuals, busy professionals, and fitness enthusiasts seeking a hassle-free and balanced approach to nutrition.

Market Analysis and Competition - Understand Your Market

Demonstrate a thorough analysis of your target market and provide evidence of the demand for your offerings. Include information about the market size, projected customer base, and repeat customer potential. Discuss your competition and outline how your business will differentiate itself.

Product or Service - Describe Your Core Offering

Provide a detailed explanation of the product or service at the core of your business. Remember to present it as if you were describing it to someone who is completely new to the idea. Avoid assuming prior knowledge and ensure clarity in your description.

Marketing and Sales Plan - Reach Your Target Market

Outline your strategies for reaching your target market. Will you create a website and establish social media profiles? Are you planning to attend trade shows? Consider paid advertising options as well. Don't limit your plans to the initial stage; mention any future marketing efforts.

Ownership, Management, and Personnel - Organize Your Team

Describe how you will manage and staff your business. Discuss the ownership structure if there are multiple owners and outline the types of personnel you will require. Include information about team members you plan to hire and provide a brief profile of existing key team members, including yourself.

Financial Plan and Projections - Plan Your Finances

This section is vital for both your own planning and potential investor considerations. Develop a cash flow projection detailing your monthly revenue and expenses. Create a break-even analysis to determine the number of sales required to cover expenses and generate profit. Use anticipated values to construct a sample profit-and-loss statement and include a balance sheet depicting your business's current assets, liabilities, and equity.

Investment - Outline Investor Returns

Specify what investors will receive based on your cash flow projections. This includes outside investors you may approach in the future and anyone who has already invested in the business formation, such as yourself and current team members.

Appendices - Supportive Data

Gather any supporting data relevant to your business and include it in the appendices section. This can consist of testimonials, research excerpts, charts, and other pertinent information that adds credibility and depth to your business plan.

Choosing a Platform for Your Online Business

Chintan Shah (2022), a serial entrepreneur and the current

CEO of *Brainvire*, says that selecting the ideal e-commerce platform for your business is akin to building a strong foundation for a house. It plays a pivotal role in determining the value you derive from your hosting service. Each platform comes with its own set of features, advantages, and costs. However, opting for an ill-suited platform can result in squandered budgets, additional expenses, and missed chances for expansion.

Conversely, dedicating thoughtful consideration to selecting the right platform can yield numerous benefits. These include establishing a dependable online presence, delivering a seamless user experience, generating leads swiftly, and boosting your ROI.

Shah suggested five things you can consider when choosing a platform for your online business:

1. Robust Security Measures:

- Ensure the platform offers SSL certification, fraud prevention, data backups, and PCI compliance to protect customer privacy and data.

- Opt for platforms built on object-oriented programming languages for enhanced security protocols.

2. SEO Capabilities:

- Prioritize platforms that facilitate easy optimization of

content for search engines.

- Look for features like customizable URLs, metadata management, and options for adding blogs and customer reviews.

3. Responsive Website Design:

- Embrace a responsive web design to cater to the growing number of customers using smartphones and other devices during purchase.

- Ensure your e-commerce store is accessible and user-friendly across different devices, including laptops, smartphones, and tablets.

4. Scalability:

- Choose an e-commerce platform that can scale alongside your business growth.

- Even if your store is small initially, plan for future expansion and select a platform capable of accommodating increased traffic and functionality.

5. Omnichannel Marketing:

- Leverage platforms that support omnichannel marketing to reach customers through various channels.

- Enhance customer engagement, retention, conversion rates, and revenue by utilizing multiple marketing channels seamlessly.

Building a Website

Of Course! You need a website. A good and effective one at that. If you want to generate lots of traffic for your product or service through your website, you should consider these. The points here are not elaborate, but they'll get you started.

1. Obtain a good domain name

- Make it easy to spell

- Keep it short

- Use the proper domain extension (.com)

- Avoid numbers and hyphens

- Make the address broad for future growth

- Ensure it is memorable

- Research the domain name

- Check the price

- Choose a name that conveys meaning

- Create an SEO-friendly URL

2. Purchase secure, scalable website hosting with good tech support

- Avoid shared hosting

- Dedicated server hosting is expensive but optimal

- Consider a virtual private server (VPS) hosting plan

- Look for phone and chat support

- Ensure an easy-to-use server interface

- Check server security and backups

3. Prominently display a clear description of your business

- Use the main homepage banner and introductory text

- Provide easily accessible "About Us" page links

4. Implement the best content management system (CMS). These are options you can consider:

- **WordPress:** popular and flexible, but has security issues

- **Drupal:** secure but less extensible than WordPress

- Joomla!: better SEO and security than WordPress, but not as extensible

- Squarespace: easy "drag and drop" experience, suitable for creatives

- Wix: user-friendly and quick to publish a site

5. Choose a good e-commerce platform

- WooCommerce: popular WordPress plugin for online stores

- Shopify: standalone platform with easy setup and management

- Shopify Plus: offers customization, staff accounts, and international options

- Business Squarespace: e-commerce subscription for Squarespace users

- Wix: has a Shopify extension for user-friendly e-commerce

- GoDaddy Online Store: easy setup and use with templates

6. Create an interesting, memorable, and engaging website user interface

- Use beautiful graphics and easy-to-read fonts

- Optimize graphics for fast loading

- Research competition and target audience

- Stay consistent with your brand

- Design intuitive navigation

- Publish easily accessible contact information

- Incorporate obvious call-to-actions

- Include standard pages (Home, About Us, Products/Services, etc.)

7. Optimize your small business website for search engines

- Conduct keyword research and implementation

- Optimize website code

- Ensure fast loading speed

- Implement SSL certificate for security

- Have a mobile-friendly site

- Obtain high-quality backlinks

- Encourage positive reviews

- Use internal links and social media for promotion

Creating Contents that Sell

Did you ever watch one of those old-fashioned TV adverts where two people talk about the amazing benefits of a particular product? One of them lists the benefits of the products, and the other person's job is to exclaim in awe to show how awesome the product is. I have to tell you, watching those things leaves me in a heap of laughter because the 'Wows' of surprise and awe are so dramatic!

But I won't judge you if you choose to exclaim in awe when you find out that you'll be learning about other useful AI tools apart from ChatGPT. I know I promised to talk only about ChatGPT, but what kind of friend will I be if I don't give you the best? Feel free to exclaim as much as you want.

We now know that ChatGPT can help you run your business successfully, but you also know about its limitations, so there are several things it can't do. We'll need to consider other AI tools that will help simplify your journey and make it easier to run your side hustle.

There are a lot of AI apps and tools already in the market with a lot more popping up each day, but here are the essentials you'll need:

1. Canva

But Canva isn't a new tool and has been around the block for quite a while, right? That's correct, but their text-to-image AI feature has taken things a step further. You can create stunning pieces of art in a few minutes with a good text prompt. You can create unique images for your social media content, flyers, and so on. Plus you can also edit and add text to your image right there in Canva. Check it out; you won't regret it.

2. Lumen5

It's no news that video content converts a lot more than text-based content or still images. That means you need to create videos to help market your products. I don't know about you, but putting together a cohesive video can be more than a little stressful and time-consuming. Enter Lumen5. It's an AI-powered platform that helps you create stellar video content in a matter of minutes. It has templates you can personalize to fit your brand outlook and images, video clips, and even music to keep things interesting. You can create a video in about 10 to 15 minutes while saving time and money.

All you simply have to do is to add a link to the blog article or website with the content you'd like transformed into a video. Alternatively, you can put in some text. The AI platform converts it into a video, and boom! You're in business. It has a free version, but you'll have to pay to get access to some features.

3. Looka

Need to create your logo and brand kit but just don't know where to start, or you're not especially creative? Looka is an AI-powered platform that helps you create a logo and a brand kit. I'm talking about business card designs, email signatures, letterheads, invoices, social media post templates, and so much more. You can also get an AI-generated website too if you'd like.

You'll get to input the details you'd like to see as well as your preferences. After a series of short, easy steps, you'll have created your logo, and you can even go ahead to have it customized on your brand materials and social media kit. It runs on a paid subscription, but you can also pay for one-time usage.

4. Legal Robot

One aspect of running a business that's often overlooked is the legal aspect. I'd hate you to make all that money only to lose it because you didn't follow due process. Legal robot is an AI that helps you make sense of legal documents. It's great for analyzing contracts, simplifying complicated legal terms, and ensuring that your business is fully compliant with the law.

These are only a few tools, but they are great if you're starting. Don't hesitate to learn more and try out more AI tools because, as I always say, the possibilities are endless! One certain thing is that with the right complement of AI tools, running your business will get easier as you progress. I'd also like to add that while AI does a lot of the work for you, you can't let it run unsupervised. The point of automation is to cut down your working hours, but when you get started, you may have to dedicate more time to the process. As soon as you get the hang of things, you'll be able to cut down your weekly working hours, and this book is here to show you how to achieve that in the fastest way possible.

Chapter Five

Staying Ahead of The Game

"To become financially independent you must turn part of your income into capital; turn capital into enterprise; turn enterprise into profit; turn profit into investment; and turn investment into financial independence."
– Jim Rohn

My friend Peter loves dogs, and he's very attached to Lassie, his golden retriever. Yes, yes, it's Lassie, like the movie. I know. What can I say? He really loves dogs.

He's had Lassie trained by a bunch of expert dog trainers, so she's the most well-behaved doggo in the universe. Yeah, she's a good girl. We took her to a dog show last summer, and Pete entered her into the contest, and she did a great job. That is until she got to the last stage of the show where she had to complete an obstacle course along with three other finalists. She started well, jumping over hoops and climbing through the little tunnels. She was well ahead of the others until she screeched to a halt and froze!

Uh oh. "*Lassie! Here girl*!" Peter hollered at the top of his voice from the finish line, but she gave him a brief distracted look and kept staring into the audience. Pete and I looked at each other because we knew what that strangely intent look on her face meant. We looked around, and sure enough, someone was unwrapping what looked like a sandwich in the stands, right beside where Lassie was standing. She loved sandwiches, but she loved PB and J sandwiches the most. She turned around, went up to the stands, rose on her hind legs, and stared at the lady with the sandwich with big, gooey, brown eyes. Thankfully, the lady found her charming and fed her a bit of her sandwich. Of course, Lassie decided to sit right there and wait for more.

Needless to say, she lost the race, but she won the audience's hearts and still got a medal for being a very good girl. I think a video of her at the show went viral on YouTube. If you ever encountered something like that, that was Lassie!

Now that you have a pretty good idea of how you can use AI to set up your various passive income streams for success, you need to learn one very important factor, or else you'll end up just like Lassie, settling for the immediate gain and losing out on the future prize. We certainly do not want that. I think we can both agree that the AI industry moves very fast, and

I'm sure we'll be talking about fully independent self-driving cars by 2030. So you need to learn how to stay current with the trends, how to upgrade your AI, where to go for the latest news in the industry, and how to avoid making mistakes with AI.

I think you should practice what you learn in this chapter as soon as you can. You don't need to wait until you set up a successful business when you start. I'm not psychic, but I can almost predict that a lot of money you'll make will be from the fact that you had access to the right information early enough and acted on it. That's how we win in this game, by moving fast.

AI in E-commerce

What's the strangest thing you've ever bought online? Or better yet, what's the weirdest thing you can find online? I did a little search, and here are a few wild things I found for sale on Amazon:

- Coyote urine

- Hand underpants

- A ghost meter, yes, for detecting ghosts

- Edible insects

- Tiny hands puppets for your fingers

The hilarious thing is that each of these products has at least 50 ratings on Amazon, with some having as many as 800 ratings! (Yes, you guessed right, it was the hand underpants.) So, if you're starting an E-comm business and worried no one will buy, relax.

E-commerce, which is basically buying and selling online, has really come a long way, and now thanks to AI, we're just getting started. Right off the bat, one of the key benefits of AI in e-commerce is that it can complete numerous activities that a person would typically complete, but much faster and more accurately. Add this to the fact that it can do stuff like data mining, picture recognition, and detecting anomalies in systems and processes. The best part is that it never gets tired, distracted, or bored.

Choosing to incorporate AI into your e-comm business means you can do a range of things like predicting customer buying habits, utilizing their inventory, evaluating user feedback, and increasing sales. If you're wondering how a big E-comm company can retain their clients successfully, get new ones, and keep them satisfied and loyal to the brand, I'm pretty sure AI is involved. The secret behind it all is collecting and evaluating real-time data that allows for the best customer experience.

Let's look at how you can adopt AI in e-commerce:

1. Pricing

When it comes to AI and pricing, several variables and inputs need to be considered. These include manual competitive analysis and calculations. You can use AI to implement a pricing plan that is flexible and adaptable to your business's unique profit goals. You can also customize the prices and deals you offer to visitors on your website.

One hack I like is raising prices when your supply is low. This can be a good strategy to encourage customers who need your goods right away to pay more to get them from you instead of waiting for your competitors to restock.

2. Inventory and data management

As you may know, running an e-commerce website involves managing a large amount of data daily. This includes keeping track of things like daily sales, inventory levels, returns, customer information, buying habits, and the total number of orders and successful deliveries. AI can help you better understand how your company is performing so that you can make informed decisions about areas that need improvement.

With AI-enabled inventory management, you can maintain

your stock levels based on sales trends from previous years, projected changes in product demands, and potential supply-related issues that could affect your inventory levels. You can also create personalized recommendations for each user as a business owner.

3. Chatbots

I'm sure you know that chatbots can be a valuable asset for your e-commerce business. They let your customers ask pertinent questions and receive instant answers through AI-powered technology. They can act as customer service representatives and even provide tips to make the shopping experience smoother for your customer.

Chatbots are invaluable when it's time to scale your operations, so you should invest in one as early as possible. They can gather valuable data and provide round-the-clock assistance to users. All in all, they contribute significantly to an enhanced overall user experience. Great chatbots to use are ManyChat and LivePerson.

4. Simplifying the search process for customers

AI systems can use natural language processing to understand a shopper's meaning, correct misspellings, add synonyms, or automatically add missing terms. It can also extract a category or concept the search might represent before sending the query to the search engine. This helps shoppers use more natural language or dialogue-style terms instead of precise keywords. If you've ever been on one of those websites that seem to bring up excellent search results even when your keywords are wacky, this is why.

5. Personalized shopping experience for your customers

Applying artificial intelligence (AI) and machine learning allows valuable user insights to be derived from consumer data. You can analyze customer data from multiple touchpoints, such as mobile apps, email campaigns, and websites, to measure how users interact online. With these insights, you can make suitable product recommendations and provide a consistent digital experience across all devices as a digital retailer.

This way, it recommends products tailored to your customer's preferences. For instance, it can provide behavioral recommendations by showing products other customers have viewed or bought. It can also give shopper-focused personalized suggestions based on their browsing history. It can even offer content similarity ideas by suggesting products with adjacent features or benefits. Pretty cool, right? AI tools like Vue.ai, Namogoo, and Phrasee are quite handy here.

6. Writing product descriptions

When running an E-commerce business, it's important to have product descriptions that act as a helpful shop assistant for your customers. This way, they can easily confirm if the product features match their preferences before purchasing. With AI, you can create unique and dynamic product descriptions in no time! If you're looking for a quicker and more efficient way to write a compelling product description, this method might be just what you need. It's less time-consuming than the traditional approach, which can take quite a bit of time. You can use tools like ChatGPT, Jasper, and Copyai for this.

7. Security and fraud detection

You should be aware that the E-commerce industry is vulnerable to cyber-attacks because it's very reliant on online buying and selling of goods. If sensitive personal information is exposed, it can put your customers at risk. This can also harm your reputation, so you need to pay attention to this.

With AI, you can easily identify fraudulent activity and prevent data breaches that could potentially put sensitive corporate and consumer information at risk. You need to be able to guarantee secure payment to your customers, so you'll have to make sure your website and apps are strongly encrypted.

You also want to look out for forged and fake reviews because they can sink your business faster than you imagine. Negative reviews will cause a decline in your customer base, sales revenue, and business profitability. Since your customers may not have direct contact with online sellers, they will likely rely on product reviews and ratings when purchasing. With Artificial Intelligence, you can address and remove fake reviews that may impact customer purchasing decisions. Authentic comments solely from actual customers will be left behind on the e-commerce platform. Some AI tools that are great for fraud detection are SHIELD and Forter.

8. Sales prediction

E-commerce firms can leverage artificial intelligence to generate precise sales predictions and anticipate forthcoming market trends. This can be achieved through data analysis, examination of historical data, and investigation of past and present e-commerce patterns, among other methods. You'll be able to get the data required to enhance your operations and insights to know what product to stock up on and what not to sell anymore.

9. Customer after-sale support

Nobody likes feeling like they've been abandoned after spending their hard-earned money on your product. I understand this perfectly; that's why I tell all my readers to contact me directly via email if they have any questions, comments, or concerns. You should be able to offer something similar for your e-comm business.

With AI, you can ask customers to provide feedback, show them how to use the product and tell them about your return policies or what to do if they aren't satisfied with the product.

10. Content production

Any business owner who sells a wide variety of physical products online will tell you that taking pictures of the products and editing them to look good enough to shop is the most stressful thing ever. Thanks to AI, there's no need to fret anymore because you can enhance your pictures with a single tap of your fingers thanks to the AI optimization option available on most editing apps. You can also generate life-like videos and photos known as deep fakes for your products. You can use AI to create voice overs that provide useful information for your buyers. The aim is to reduce the hassle, expense, and wasted effort of traditional content creation.

Your customers should be able to get personalized product recommendations, and orders placed for them with AI, strong customer service, and after-sales support. They should also be able to search with images. If you sell homewares and furniture, you can even offer Augmented Reality and Virtual Reality options so your clients can see what the product looks like in their home.

If you don't have those things in place yet, you can work toward achieving them, but the overall goal is to keep your customers satisfied and happy.

Latest AI Trends and Updates

You'll need to be deliberate about staying up to date with industry trends. That means you need to have a good idea of what's happening right now and what may happen. You'll be able to anticipate changes and take the right action to protect your brand or business. With that being said, let's look at the trends in the AI industry that you should be aware of:

1. Cybersecurity

We're already seeing this, and we'll most likely see more of it as we go along. As cybercrime becomes more of a concern for businesses, AI is being deployed more often in cybersecurity and surveillance. Access security mechanisms, such as face and voice recognition, video analysis, and biometric identification, will be augmented by employing AI algorithms that can learn to identify and flag illegal conduct before it becomes a problem.

On the flip side, this means that hackers may also experience a reduction in the total time to deploy a cyber-attack, thanks to AI. This automatically means that the cybersecurity industry will need more people with the right expertise to be employed. Security AI, managed by experts, may also handle essential parts of cybersecurity like data management, vulnerability assessment, and threat detection.

In 2022, IBM found that companies with established procedures for managing cyber risk saved an average of USD3 million and cut breach lifecycles by 74 days, thanks to early identification and remediation (IBM, 2022). This also allows the insurance industry to implement personalized policies to help with cyber risk assessment and management.

2. Ethics and regulations

For many years, the AI business has been largely unchecked by government oversight because no legislation or regulation was in place to guide its growth and use. However, this is starting to change as governments worldwide set up frameworks for more AI regulation.

There's still a long way to go, especially in the field of generative AI like ChatGPT, where several programs are being accused of breaching copyright laws by harvesting artists' work off the internet without their permission. There's a rising demand for a more transparent and ethical AI algorithm. People want to know how these technologies are developed, distributed, and used. There are also concerns about the data used to train these systems because some biases have already been spotted. This is important because, for instance, companies that use AI to screen potential recruits need to have a transparent process to ensure that their AI algorithm isn't ignoring a particular race or gender.

3. Healthcare

The healthcare industry has started the adoption of AI technology. Healthcare practitioners have found AI helpful since it allows them to better support patient care. With the increased use of AI and robotics, we can see there's an improvement in the efficiency and availability of safe medical treatment for people. We saw the start of large-scale adoption of AI during the Covid-19 pandemic with devices like thermal cameras for sensing patient temperatures and contactless delivery tools. As AI improves the efficiency of electronic health records, doctors can provide more precise diagnostics, create more individualized medications, and craft more individualized treatment plans for their patients.

AI has also been used to streamline the process of obtaining up-to-the-minute information from medical records. This allows for quicker diagnosis and better care overall. Moreover, AI is helping hospital employees properly manage patient data, new admissions, and other tasks.

Let's not forget about wearable devices and their potential uses for telemedicine. Health care practitioners may be able to examine patients remotely one day. Emotional AI helps youngsters with autism, sad people, and those with degenerative diseases like dementia interact with the world around them. There are a lot of possibilities here, and watching each of them get explored will be very exciting, don't you think?

4. Increased Human and AI Collaboration

Collaborative robots, or cobots, have attained and will continue to reach unprecedented levels of AI assistance for various human tasks. Experts predict that more businesses will use machines equipped with artificial intelligence to handle routine, physically demanding jobs, freeing up workers for higher-value roles.

In addition to enhancing safety and reducing repair and injury costs, AI features may help teams discover and respond quickly to problems and failures. These devices can be used to help companies with supply chain problems and shortages of workers. Perhaps it's not a reach to assume that robots will eventually take over the workforce when you consider how much they can do and how well. We've got AI here creating Oscar-worthy works of art and mainly giving accurate medical diagnoses.

We may not have to worry much about that because AI aims to make work easier, not replace humans entirely. But I'll admit that we need to take a strong, regulatory approach to ensure the AI is created with this end in mind.

5. Generative artificial intelligence will be the object of much focus and become increasingly smarter

This subfield of machine learning focuses on generating new data or content. Deep learning algorithms can be applied to almost any type of data, including code, text, photos, audio, video, etc., to reveal hidden patterns and characteristics. The star of our show, ChatGPT, falls squarely into this category. As a result of ChatGPT, several other generative AI models have emerged, including viral AI art generators like DALL-E 2 and Midjourney, expanding the boundaries of what was previously thought possible with artificial intelligence.

This means that generative AI technologies will need to improve their ethics and security if businesses are going to feel comfortable adopting and working with them.

6. Increased use of low-code and no-code tools

You may not know this, but back then, we had to hire developers who'd painstakingly write long lines of code to build stuff. Now, thanks to AI, you can use many low-code and no-code tools to build apps and other tools.

This is great news for organizations and small business owners like you who want to use advanced technology without investing heavily in staff training. These tools will make building AI systems and other apps easy because they mostly have drag-and-drop components and other no-code tools.

7. AI and voice technology

Voice biometrics, voice authentication, voice cloning, content localization, and no-code AI platforms are all examples of how

AI is being used in the field of voice technology.

In speech biometrics, a voice assistant takes a recording of a person's voice and uses it to create a "voiceprint" against which every new voice it hears may be judged. By recreating an individual's voice from a sample, voice cloning speeds up the process of creating voice-overs for media like movies and video games. This means that businesses may use voice cloning to localize material so that customers can hear advertisements or instructions in their original language, and directors can change an actor's voice to sound like they're speaking a different language.

8. Self-driving cars

To be honest, I'm personally interested in having self-driving cars out there because how cool would that be? There's been a rise in the use of artificial intelligence-based driver monitoring systems in cars, which may detect tiredness or sickness and either notify human drivers or activate autonomous driving. These cars will also have adaptive cruise controls, which can issue alerts and modify the vehicle's speed before a potential accident. This is because technology like sensors and radars for object identification and convolutional neural networks for terrain recognition and classification continues to improve. There's speculation that these cars will be able to communicate with other autonomous vehicles to prevent collisions with pedestrians, stationary objects, and other vehicles.

9. AI and business automation

More and more companies are turning to AI-based automation systems to improve efficiency. Among the possible automation applications here are marketing campaigns, appointment settings, and more. Human data processes are being replaced by automation. Artificially intelligent machines are on track to memorize and repeat particular tasks theoretically. The bonus is that human error is minimized or eliminated, and stress levels among workers are lowered as a result.

10. Explainable AI

AI has improved in recent years but can still be biased or misused. This has spurred the development of a new area of study called explainable AI, in which scientists analyze AI models' patterns mathematically to determine how the systems make their judgments.

The National Institute of Standards defines four principles of explainable AI: that the system only operates under the conditions it was designed for, or when the system reaches sufficient confidence in its output; that the explanations for all outputs are understandable to individual users; that the explanation accurately reflects the process used to arrive at that output; and that the system only operates under the conditions it was designed for.

Knowing what's happening in the industry may be difficult to follow because of the technical terms and intricate contexts. The good news is that you can ask ChatGPT to explain anything you find difficult. I know; you literally cannot lose out here!

How to Stay Updated

When did you last hear or use the word "obsolete"? Well, I looked it up on SEMrush, an AI keyword research tool, and I found that this word has just about 60k search volume in about seven days compared to "AI," which has over 200k. This means that most internet users aren't reading about the *obsolescence syndrome*—don't try looking it up, it's my coinage—that comes with the age of AI, yet the fear of getting displaced from jobs is eating up many people.

In this instance, I think fear is misplaced. If there is anything to worry about, it's becoming "obsolete." This word isn't trendy, but that's what is happening to individuals and businesses out there. Some folks are becoming obsolete in their fields because they're not on board with the highball technological shifts in town. Businesses are losing relevance for the same reason.

If you don't want to become like one of those *ol' people* who refused to move with past industrial revolutions, here's how you can stay up-to-date.

1. Utilize Online Resources to Stay Informed

Keeping up with trends in your industry can be a breeze if you know where to look. One of the easiest ways is to follow online resources offering up-to-date news, insightful commentary, helpful tutorials, and engaging courses on AI in your industry. You can sign up for newsletters, blogs, podcasts, YouTube channels, and online magazines that cover your industry's latest gist, especially involving AI, from various angles and levels of complexity.

Get acquainted with platforms that are specific to your industry. Some general platforms, such as Medium, Reddit, and Quora, can also be useful for staying up to date. You can read and write articles, ask and answer questions, and join discussions on AI in your industry. It's a fun and interactive way to connect with other AI enthusiasts and learn more about the subject.

Patricia C. (2023), a solution architect, shared one of the ways she stays up-to-date on her LinkedIn page. She said that she tends to listen to audiobooks, which provide her with various perspectives from different types of people, such as AI engineers, software developers, businesspeople, and more.

2. Network with Colleagues and Industry Leaders

You shouldn't underestimate the power of networking as you strive to stay updated. No. Don't! Connecting with colleagues and leaders in your industry can give you access to valuable knowledge, experience, and feedback that can help you grow your skills. There's always something to learn from others' successes and challenges.

If you're looking for guidance or mentorship, reaching out to an expert in the field can be incredibly beneficial. They can help you develop your skills and advance your business. Don't be afraid to leverage platforms like LinkedIn, Twitter, and Slack to connect with others in your community. These platforms can be great resources for building relationships and expanding your knowledge.

3. Maintain a Curious and Open-Mindset

I stressed the role of curiosity in one of my books on AI. I perceive curiosity as the common denominator for all forms of innovation we've ever witnessed on our planet. People keep asking questions; that's what led them to carry out research on what could be that hasn't been yet.

Don't let your curiosity fade when it comes to the possibilities and implications of AI! Keep asking questions and seeking answers; that's how you stay ahead of the game. It's also important to stay mindful of AI's ethical, social, and economic aspects and how they can impact you and your business.

Thankfully, plenty of resources are out there to help you stay informed and inspired. Platforms like TED, WIRED, and The Conversation offer a wealth of inspiring and thought-provoking stories and opinions on AI. So keep your mind open, and keep exploring the exciting world of AI!

Avoiding Common AI Mistakes

It's really important to use AI in customer service these days, but you need to be careful not to make mistakes that could end up being really expensive. If you mess it up, it could hurt the experience for the people using the service and make it harder to get a good return on your AI investment.

I've curated ten common mistakes individuals and organizations make with AI. I'll tell you how to avoid them afterward.

10 common AI mistakes you should avoid

1. Not having a clear understanding of the problem you're trying to solve with AI

2. Using biased or incomplete data to train the AI model

3. Overfitting the model to the training data can result in poor performance on new data

4. Underestimating the amount of data required to train an accurate AI model

5. Failing to validate the performance of the AI model on new data

6. Assuming that AI can solve all problems and neglecting the importance of human expertise

7. Neglecting to consider the ethical implications and potential negative consequences of AI applications

8. Failing to plan for ongoing maintenance and updates to the AI model

9. Trying to implement AI in areas where it may not be the best solution

10. Assuming that AI will be a quick fix for complex problems and underestimating the time and effort

required for successful implementation.

How to avoid AI mistakes

❖ **Find the Perfect Mix of Human and Automated Customer Service**

Using AI in customer service is meant to make customers happier. By responding more quickly and fixing issues faster, AI has become a popular tool in customer support. But customers really feel valued when they get a personal touch. So how do we make interactions more personal? Well, AI is getting better at analyzing past interactions, preferences, and demographics. However, relying too much on technology and not enough on human interaction can sometimes make customers feel overwhelmed.

That's why, when you want to implement AI in your operations, it's important to find the right balance and use AI only where necessary. It's important to use AI to make things easier while still keeping a personal touch. It's wise to take advantage of AI's capabilities without forgetting the importance of human interaction.

❖ **Understand the Importance of Maintaining and Monitoring AI**

Don't ever let this out of your mind: deploying an AI model is just the beginning. To keep improving results, you need to train the model continuously. And as your AI project gets more complex, the risk of failure also increases. That's why it's crucial to allocate resources for maintaining and monitoring your AI projects right from the planning stage.

Don't wait until something goes wrong before thinking about maintenance and monitoring. Make it a priority right from the start to ensure the success of your AI projects.

❖ Measure the Performance of your AI

AI isn't as perfect as you think. It needs to be checked too. Measuring the performance of your AI is as essential as measuring the performance of your employees. Unfortunately, many organizations fail to recognize the return on investment from AI implementations. Either they don't assess the project properly or use the wrong assessment methodology.

AI often replicates human behavior in customer service, so it's important to measure its performance against customer satisfaction levels and how well it mimics human behavior.

By measuring AI's performance regularly and using the right methodology, you can ensure that you get the most out of your AI projects and deliver the best customer experience possible.

❖ Train your employees

Just as you're thinking about replacing your employees with

chatbots and other AI services, there's something you should consider before you jump into it: training.

You might be thinking, "Why would I need training if the chatbots are doing all the work?" However, it is important to remember that not all tasks can be automated. Only routine tasks will be automated. That's why it's super important to start sharing knowledge with your employees to improve the whole process with chatbots and AI.

So, don't skip out on the training. It will help you make the most of your new AI systems and ensure that your employees are on board with the changes.

❖ Incorporate Self-Service Options in Your Chatbot Strategy

I consider improper planning the biggest mistake organizations make when implementing chatbots. They just go ahead and deploy chatbots without any real thought about how they'll fit into the bigger picture. So, before you even think about chatbots, you need to plan out the resources you'll need, which processes you want to automate, and what options you want to provide your customers.

One key thing that organizations often overlook is self-service options. Make sure you include these in your plan for chatbot implementation. With that in place, your customers can get the help they need quickly and easily.

❖ Use Data to Improve Your Chatbot Experience

If you want to offer the best customer experience with your chatbot, you need to keep learning and improving. It's not a one-time task that you can just set and forget. Instead, you need to leverage data to analyze customer interactions and offer feedback to improve continuously.

Haricharan (2022), a digital marketer and digital transformation strategist, believes that without analyzing previous chat interactions, your customers might find the chatbot experience overwhelming. So, make sure you're taking advantage of data to improve the chatbot's interactions.

Learning from the mistakes of others and avoiding them is a sure path to success in this industry. That's a way of telling you to pay close attention to some organizations' common mistakes with implementing AI and the possible ways to avoid them.

Chapter Recap

This chapter explored how AI is changing the e-commerce landscape, including the latest trends and updates. I shared with you the importance of staying up to date with these trends and offered tips for how to do so. I also pointed out ten common mistakes businesses make when implementing AI in e-commerce and shared strategies for avoiding these pitfalls.

By leveraging the power of AI and staying informed about the latest developments in this industry, your e-commerce business can gain a competitive advantage and deliver superior customer experiences.

PART THREE

SCALING AND OPTIMIZING SALES

As you approach the final part of this book, you have already learned a great deal about artificial intelligence and the amazing benefits it offers to the human community. Now, it's time to take your side hustle to the next level by focusing on how AI can enhance your business to maximize profits. In this section, you will discover effective strategies to scale your business and increase your revenue streams with AI tools

One of the key components of growing your side hustle is marketing. In the second chapter of this section, you will learn how to automate your marketing strategies to optimize your sales. You can reach a wider audience and convert more leads into paying customers by leveraging technology and data-driven approaches. You will explore different tools and techniques to streamline your marketing efforts and increase conversion rates.

As with any business, there will always be risks and challenges that you may encounter along the way. In the final chapter of this section, you will learn how to troubleshoot and solve common problems that can arise in your side hustle.

By the end of this section, you will have a comprehensive understanding of how to scale your side hustle and maximize your profits. With the strategies and techniques you will learn, you can take your business to the next level and achieve your desired success.

So, let's dive in and explore the world of scalable side hustles!

Chapter Six

Scaling your Side Hustle

There are no downsides to a side hustle. There are only benefits to building more than one source of income.
—Forbes

I was at an international business conference recently where the main speaker shared the story of a countryside farmer who did a thing to scale his business.

Jack owned a small farm in the countryside. He loved farming but struggled to make a living with his small plot of land. He dreamed of expanding his farm but didn't know how to go about it. One day, Jack decided to seek the advice of a wise old farmer in the nearby town. The wise old farmer listened to Jack's struggles and offered him a metaphorical lesson.

"Jack," the old farmer said, "scaling up your farm is like planting a seed. You need to prepare the soil, plant the seed, water it, and nurture it until it grows into a healthy plant."

Jack was confused, but the wise old farmer continued, "To prepare the soil, you need to do your research and find the right location for your farm. Once you have the land, you need to invest in the necessary equipment and resources to plant the seed.

"Watering the seed is like investing in your business. You must allocate your resources wisely, hire the right people, and invest in technology and infrastructure to help your business grow.

"And finally, nurturing the plant is like building your brand and reputation. You need to provide excellent customer service, deliver high-quality products or services, and establish trust with your customers and stakeholders."

Jack was amazed by the wisdom of the old farmer. By implementing the old farmer's advice, his farm grew into a successful business that provided for him and his family.

We can learn and apply a few things from the old farmer's advice to Jack. Scaling up in any business, even if you call it a side hustle, is like planting a seed. It takes time, effort, and patience, but your side hustle can become a successful enterprise with the right strategy and mindset. As you can tell, AI is the main strategy I've been brandishing in this book. Let's see how AI can help your side hustle scale up.

Creating a Growth Strategy

A guest writer on *WordStream* admitted that running a business can sometimes be a daunting challenge for a small business owner, a marketing team, or an agency. One of the reasons for this is that it's not always easy to anticipate what's coming next or to set realistic goals. That's what makes having a growth strategy essential for any business. It allows you to plan for success and set achievable goals.

This strategy is primarily meant for anyone wanting long-term business growth. That said, it's important to remember that growth isn't always steady or immediate. It takes time and planning to achieve sustainable growth. So, it's essential to be prepared and plan accordingly, even with AI.

Growth is growth anywhere. The strategy might differ, but the result is usually the same. The traditional ways of growing a business are still relevant in the AI age. AI only enhances it and makes growth happen quicker by using data-driven insights to identify opportunities and potential obstacles and leveraging AI-powered tools to optimize decision-making and execution.

1. Revisit your business goal

One of the first steps in creating a growth strategy for your business is defining your goals. But this time, I want to assume you already have an objective, either in your head or written, but it's best written. What you need to do is revisit it. But if you don't have one yet, you can take the liberty to create one before moving on.

If you don't have any goals in place, your business will have no specific direction, and in the worst-case scenario, the business will be grounded in a matter of months. Therefore, it's essential to have a clear understanding of what you want to achieve so that you can develop a plan to get there.

For example, your goal might be to increase sales by a certain percentage, expand into new markets, or improve customer retention rates. Once you have your goals in place, you'll need to determine which metrics and data points are most relevant to tracking your progress. These might include website traffic, customer satisfaction ratings, or revenue growth.

These are just the pieces of information you need to take your side hustle to the next level. However, to understand all the data you've been collecting, AI tools will come in handy to help you make sense of it. AI tools will help you spot patterns, predict future trends, and make informed decisions based on the data.

When you have clear goals in mind and know which metrics to track, you can create a growth strategy that's laser-focused and effective. It's all about using data to guide you in the right direction and achieve your objectives.

2. Incorporate Customer Feedback

Ed Calnan (cited by Forbes, 2021) of *Seismic* says your customers are key to your business's growth. So listening to them and incorporating their feedback into your growth strategy is crucial. Happy customers are more likely to stick with you, refer others to your business, and buy more of your products and services.

But gathering and analyzing customer feedback can be time-consuming and challenging. That's where AI comes in. AI-powered tools can quickly and accurately analyze customer feedback data, identify trends, and provide insights to guide your growth strategy.

By leveraging AI, you can streamline the process of incorporating customer feedback into your growth strategy. This, in turn, can help you keep your customers happy and grow your business more effectively.

3. Try automation

Having a job that fetches you a regular income is demanding on its own. Now to run another business on the side, it takes a whole lot more. This means that you have a million things to do every day. You shouldn't make life more difficult for yourself by sticking with manual business methods; AI can help you with most tasks and make life easier for you.

With AI, you can automate many of those time-consuming, manual processes. Implementing AI-powered automation tools can streamline your business operations and improve efficiency.

I know we've mentioned this previously; let's go over what AI can do again. AI can help with tasks like customer service, data entry, and even scheduling. You can use AI chatbots to handle routine customer inquiries, freeing up your team to focus on more complex issues. AI can also help with data entry, automatically categorizing and organizing data so that it's easier to analyze. And with AI-powered scheduling tools, you can quickly and easily find the best times for meetings, appointments, and other events.

By automating these processes, you can free up valuable resources to reinvest in growth initiatives. You can focus on developing new products or services, expanding into new markets, or improving customer satisfaction.

So, if you want to take your business to the next level, it's time to start exploring some operations that can be automated and channeling your resources to other things to achieve your growth goals.

4. Create a New Product or Service Category and Dominate It

Let's take this a notch up. I know we're talking about growth here, but would you like to be a trailblazer in your industry? Then don't be content with just competing in an existing product or service category. Instead, create your own! That's exactly what Matt Mong of *ADEACA* (cited by Forbes, 2021) suggested. Carve out a new niche for yourself; that way, you can become the undisputed king of that category and make your competition irrelevant.

However, this won't just happen on a rollercoaster cruise. Creating a new product or service category can be a daunting task, but with the help of AI, it's easier than ever to identify unmet needs in your market and develop innovative solutions. By incorporating AI-powered tools and techniques into your growth strategy, you can gain a competitive edge and become the leader in your new category.

You can do this by using AI tools to analyze customer data to identify patterns and trends in their behavior. By understanding what your customers want and need, you can develop products and services that meet those needs and differentiate yourself from your competition.

By utilizing AI, you can enhance your marketing strategies by assessing customer engagement and determining the most efficient methods to reach your intended audience. The implementation of AI-powered tools in personalized marketing can help you deliver specific messages to individual customers, resulting in the creation of more robust customer relationships.

Another way to use AI to create a new category is by automating certain tasks, such as data entry or customer service. This can free up resources that can be reinvested in growth initiatives, such as product development or market expansion.

With the help of AI, you can create a new product or service category that meets your customers' needs and dominates your competition. So, don't be afraid to embrace AI and incorporate it into your growth strategy to achieve your goals.

If you can successfully create a new product or service category, you'll be opening up a world of potential growth for your business. So, don't be afraid to chart your own path and blaze a trail that others will follow!

5. Invest and Improve Your Sales Team's Performance

Let's see what we can make of the statistics Joe DiDonato of Baker Communications, Inc shared. He said that according to the Sales Management Association, a formal sales process could improve revenues by 18%. Additionally, organizations that invest in upskilling their sales teams by training their sellers bring in 9% more revenue, and those that spend three hours per month on pipeline management see an 11%

increase in revenues. Companies that followed all three of these best practices experienced a 28% increase in revenues.

What does this tell you?

Investing in your sales team's skills is crucial to the success of your business. If you take that further and expose them to AI-powered tools, it can take their performance to the next level. By implementing AI into your sales process, you can improve revenue and streamline operations.

AI can assist in lead scoring and prioritization, allowing your sales team to focus on high-quality leads more likely to convert. This saves time and energy that can be directed towards other aspects of the sales process. Another way AI can help is through personalized sales. With AI-powered tools, your sales team can deliver personalized messaging to each potential customer, improving engagement and increasing the likelihood of conversion.

AI can also help in forecasting and pipeline management, allowing your team to anticipate potential issues and opportunities before they arise. This proactive approach can lead to more effective decision-making and improved revenue.

So, don't hesitate to invest in your sales team's skills and incorporate AI into your sales infrastructure. Doing so can boost revenue, improve performance, and stay ahead of the competition.

6. Track Your Progress and Optimize Your Strategy with AI

Monitoring and measuring the results of your growth strategy is crucial to ensuring its success. This is where AI-powered analytics tools come in handy. They can help you analyze vast amounts of data and provide insights to inform your strategy.

One of the main benefits of AI-powered analytics tools is their ability to analyze customer behavior. By tracking data such as purchasing patterns, product preferences, and interactions with your business, you can gain valuable insights into your customers' needs and wants. This information can be used to refine your growth strategy and tailor your offerings to meet your customers' needs better.

Another way AI can help you measure your growth strategy is through predictive modeling. This involves analyzing historical data and identifying patterns that can be used to forecast future trends. By predicting how your business will perform in the future, you can make informed decisions to help you stay ahead of the competition.

Real-time data analysis is another critical benefit of AI-powered analytics tools. With the ability to analyze vast amounts of data in real time, you can identify trends and opportunities for growth quickly. This allows you to make informed decisions on the fly and pivot your strategy as needed to capitalize on emerging trends.

Personalization is another area where AI can help you measure the success of your growth strategy. By analyzing customer data, AI algorithms can help you create customized campaigns that resonate with your audience. As a result, this can potentially result in a boost in engagement, greater conversion rates, and an increase in revenue.

Overall, AI-powered analytics tools are powerful tools for measuring and monitoring the success of your growth strategy. By leveraging their insights, you can refine your strategy, make data-driven decisions, and, ultimately, drive growth for your business.

7. AI SEO Tools Can Help Improve Your Website's Visibility

Increasing your site's visibility, if you have one, can translate into growth for your side hustle. AI tools help you discover keyword opportunities and optimize your content.

One of the benefits of using AI-powered SEO tools is that they provide you with more in-depth insight into the keywords you should be targeting. By analyzing user search data, these tools can identify your business's most relevant and profitable keywords. They can also suggest link-building opportunities to help you increase your website's authority and drive more traffic.

In addition to keyword research, AI SEO tools can also help with content creation. These tools can scan the web for content created around a keyword, suggesting topics and gaps to exploit. This can save you a lot of time and effort when researching and coming up with content ideas.

Moreover, AI SEO tools can help with content optimization. They can help you create topic clusters that answer user questions, determine the optimal learning time on a given topic, and ensure that you use keywords correctly. This can help you rank higher in search results and provide a better user experience for your visitors.

Developing a Sales Funnel

Let me pique your imagination a little bit.

Imagine you're a fisherman trying to catch a big fish in the middle of a vast ocean. You cast your net wide, hoping to catch something, but you end up with a few small fish. Frustrated, you decide to change your strategy. Instead of casting your net wide, you focus on a specific spot where the big fish tend to swim.

You invest in a high-quality fishing rod and reel and use the right bait to attract the fish you want. Soon, you start seeing results. The big fish start biting, and you can reel them in one by one.

This is similar to developing a sales funnel for your business. Instead of trying to attract everyone to your product or service, you focus on a specific target market. You invest in the right tools and tactics to attract those customers, such as targeted advertising, personalized messaging, and a well-designed website that meets their needs.

When you put in all the necessary efforts to reach and retain your specific audience, your customers will become devoted to your product or service, and they'll even refer others.

So, just like the fisherman who catches the big fish by focusing on a specific spot and using the right tools, you can develop a successful sales funnel by targeting the right customers and investing in the right strategies to attract and convert them into loyal, paying customers.

What is a sales funnel?

Martin Zhel (2023), sales funnel expert and CEO at Orior Creative, describes a sales funnel as a tool businesses use to understand the process a customer goes through when buying a product or service. It's called a "funnel" because, just like a funnel, many potential customers enter at the top, but only a few make it to the bottom and purchase.

At the beginning of the sales funnel, potential customers learn about your brand and the products or services you offer. As they move down the funnel, they become more interested and may engage with your brand through emails, social media, and website visits. Eventually, they may make a purchase and become customers.

Understanding your sales funnel to improve your marketing and sales efforts is essential. By identifying where potential customers drop off in the funnel, you can focus on improving those areas and increasing the conversion rate of potential customers to actual customers.

Chapa (2021) used this simple illustration to buttress a sales funnel. Imagine your business as a physical store. You'll see people walk by, some may stop and look in, and a few might walk in the door. This marks the initial stage of the sales funnel.

Once inside, they may browse the products and select a few that catch their attention. Now, they're moving down the funnel. The customer picks a few T-shirts from the clearance rack and walks to the checkout counter. This signifies the final stage of the funnel.

If everything goes smoothly, the customer completes the purchase, and they reach the bottom of the funnel. The sales funnel is a way to visualize a potential customer's journey from discovering your business to making a purchase.

With the illustration above, we can deduce that there are different stages in a sales funnel:

#1 – Discovery

In the sales world, the first step to winning over a customer is to make them discover your product or service. This is where you catch their attention. This could happen in a variety of ways, like a social media post, a Google search, or a word-of-mouth recommendation from a friend.

At this point, the customer becomes aware of your business and what you have to offer. However, not everyone is ready to make a purchase right away. Sometimes, the customer needs more time to get to know your brand and decide if it's the right fit for them.

Think of it like a courtship – you're trying to make a good impression and convince the customer to come back for more. This is where you need to focus on building a relationship with the customer, nurturing their interest, and keeping them engaged with your business. Once you've established a strong connection, the customer is more likely to make a purchase and move further down the sales funnel.

#2 – Interest

Once consumers reach the interest stage in the sales funnel, they're likely to be exploring different options and do some research. This is your chance to shine by providing them with useful content that educates and informs them without being too *salesy*.

If you start pushing your products or services too soon, you might turn them off and scare them away. Instead, focus on establishing yourself as an expert in your field and helping your prospects make informed decisions. Offer them your assistance and show them you genuinely care about their needs and preferences.

#3 – Decision

So, your customer is finally ready to make a decision! Maybe they've already compared prices, read product reviews, and checked out your competitors. They might have even added items to their cart on your website. It's now your opportunity to close the deal.

This is your chance to show the customer why your product or service is the best choice. Make sure you're offering something special that sets you apart from the competition. It could be a limited-time discount, a free gift, or any other incentive that makes the customer say, "Yes, I want that!"

#4 – Action

The point where the consumer acts is at the bottom of the sales funnel. The bottom of the sales funnel is where the action happens. That's where the consumer finally decides to purchase your product or service and become a part of your business's community.

However, just because they bought something from you doesn't mean your job is done. The goal is to retain their interest and ensure their return for future engagements. So, your focus should be on customer retention. Make your customer feel valued by thanking them for their purchase. Encourage them to give you feedback, and let them know you are available to help with any technical issues.

Remember, customer retention is key. You want to keep them coming back and referring your business to their friends and family.

Can AI optimize sales funneling?

Definitely!

Professor John McCarthy (cited by Mishra, 2020) put AI's role in optimizing the sales funnel into words. He said that having a successful sales funnel involves many factors, like building brand awareness, enhancing the user experience, and using analytics to drive conversions. Then he asked if you've ever considered using an "intelligent machine" to take your funnel to the next level.

By utilizing AI-powered tools to closely monitor your users' behavior at every stage of the funnel, you can make smarter decisions and take the right actions to convert prospects into customers. This will help you drive conversions in your business like never before!

By building an AI sales assistant, you can enjoy a range of benefits to help you optimize your sales funnel. Check out the following list Fine (n.d.) compiled of what an AI sales assistant can do for you:

- Increase the chances of conversion by promptly following up with leads.

- Reduce the amount of time your sales team spends chasing after leads that aren't viable. A one-sided conversation with a bot can provide information to evaluate a lead's overall quality.

- Eliminate the need for manual data entry by integrating directly with your CRM software. This will enable faster customer entry into the sales funnel.

- By utilizing AI technology to follow up with customers who leave their contact information on your site, you can effectively cultivate and curate potential leads. The bot can call to confirm details, make appointments, and send relevant marketing information.

Building an Email List

One of the foremost mailing list platforms, Mailchimp (n.d), affirmed that using email marketing is a great way to connect with your customers and transform potential leads into long-term customers.

In any business, having an email list is crucial to a successful marketing campaign. With this list, you can share your brand's narrative, advertise your business, and exhibit your products to attract subscribers, ultimately turning them into loyal customers.

According to Desyllas (2022), building an email list from scratch may sound overwhelming, especially if you want to do it quickly and efficiently. But trust me; it's worth the effort in the long run because your email list will be one of your most valuable assets.

Email marketing is a tried-and-true method that can help you target your audience effectively and get a great return on investment. Desyllas affirmed that for every $1 you spend on email marketing, you can expect to get back $42 – now that's some serious ROI, isn't it?

I guess the burning question on your mind now is, "How do I build an email list?" I'll come to that shortly. But I need to remind you that everything I'm discussing here revolves around AI and how you can leverage AI tools to accomplish these tasks. I'm just letting you know that I won't just talk about building an email list; you'll also learn how AI tools can help you build one efficiently.

Here's how to go about it:

➤ **Maximizing Customer Lifecycle with AI in Email Marketing**

Vidakovic (2022) describes the customer lifecycle as the stages a customer goes through, from the moment they become aware of a product or service to when they make a purchase and eventually become a loyal, paying customer. Email marketing can play a crucial role in each stage of this process.

In the initial phase of email marketing, the focus is on recruiting potential customers. This involves building an email list by collecting email addresses from website visitors, social media followers, and other sources. With the help of AI, you can sift through a mountain of data about your customers and identify the most promising leads. This includes analyzing data such as browsing behavior, purchase history, and demographics to create targeted campaigns that speak to the needs and interests of each potential customer.

The next phase of the customer lifecycle entails communicating with prospective buyers in a way that encourages a high response rate. This involves creating engaging and relevant content that speaks to the needs and interests of the target audience. By providing valuable information, you can build trust with your subscribers and position yourself as an expert in your industry. This includes how-to guides, tips and tricks, and exclusive offers.

Once a customer has purchased, you can nurture a relationship with them through email marketing. This involves sending personalized follow-up messages that thank the customer for their purchase and provide additional resources or support. It can also include sending targeted promotions or discounts to encourage additional purchases.

At the very end of the retention process, AI can be used to re-engage dormant customers. This allows businesses to stay in constant contact with their clientele.

➤ Use AI-Generated Subject Lines

Did you know that using AI to generate email subject lines can increase open rates by 5-10%? These stats were according to Phrasee (cited by Adkuloo, 2023). According to Adkuloo, subject line generators are powered by two types of AI technologies: natural language processing (NLP) and natural language generation (NLG). NLP helps the machine read the text and convert it into machine-readable code, while NLG uses that code to generate its own words.

Big companies like Groupon and eBay have already implemented AI in their email subject lines, generating millions in revenue. You, too, can use the IBM Watson Tone Analyzer to evaluate what types of emotions and styles work best for your product or audience by running each subject line through it.

For instance, let's say you're running a clothing store and want to send out a promotional email about a new summer collection. Using AI-powered subject line generation, you could come up with something like "Get ready for summer with our new collection – 20% off today only!" The usage of compelling language, along with a call-to-action, can result in increased open rates and click-through rates. By analyzing the sentiment score and other data, you can further refine your subject lines for maximum impact.

➢ Make Your Email Content More Personalized and Interesting

No one wants to get boring, impersonal emails, especially in large batches every week. That's why email marketing strategies have evolved from batching and blasting to more personalized approaches.

Successful marketers use AI in their email marketing strategies to better segment their audience and personalize their emails. In fact, 62% of marketers believe that customized emails are the most effective strategy.

Fun and engaging emails are more likely to be opened and read – the kind you would send to your friends and family, not just customers. Personalizing your emails shows your customers that you value their unique needs.

One way in which AI can be useful is by tailoring emails to specific audience segments that exhibit similar behaviors. For instance, an AI-powered platform like Crimson could analyze your contact list and provide personalized email introductions by including pertinent updates on your recipients' industry, job role, location, and social media activities. This could result in higher engagement rates and better conversion rates for your email campaigns.

TextCortex, on the other hand, lets you compose custom emails without leaving the window you're using to send them. You can experiment with different output configurations and feature combinations until you find the one that best suits your needs.

Personalizing the opening line of your cold emails is crucial to getting responses. It shows that you've done your homework on your potential clients. Here are a few examples of personalized opening lines:

Hey there, I noticed that you recently launched a new product line. Congrats on the expansion! I think your products would really resonate with our audience, and I'd love to discuss potential partnership opportunities.

I stumbled on your blog and was impressed by the valuable content you're sharing. Your recent post on (topic) really caught my attention, and I'd love to hear more about your thoughts on the subject.

➢ Revamp Your Email Campaign Strategy

Break your email marketing campaigns down into smaller, more targeted sub-campaigns using the power of AI tools. As email privacy concerns grow, ensuring your emails get delivered to your inbox is crucial.

Take advantage of Mailmodo's automated reminder emails to entice customers who left items in their shopping carts without making a purchase. Traya achieved a 15% cart recovery rate with the help of interactive emails from Mailmodo.

AI can also help you send scheduled emails about abandoned shopping carts at specific times or in response to certain events.

Another great tool to consider is Totango's email templates. By using these templates, you can create automated, hyper-targeted email messages to enhance the customer experience and drive engagement.

➢ AI Segmentation for Better Marketing

Segmenting your email list manually is a tedious and error-prone process. That's why many marketers are turning to AI tools to automate this task.

With AI, you can use customer data such as past purchases, browsing behavior, and preferences to create segmented email lists. This allows for the sending of personalized emails to each group.

MailChimp is an excellent example of an AI tool that can provide extensive segmentation reports for any business.

AI segmentation not only improves the effectiveness of your email marketing but also saves you time and resources. You don't have to manually sort through your entire email list to identify different groups; the AI system does it for you. Plus, based on past behavior and engagement data, you can schedule automated emails to go out to specific segments at the optimal time.

Some AI-powered email marketing tools, like Omnisend, even use machine learning to constantly improve their segmentation algorithms and identify new customer segments that you may not have thought of before. This means that your email marketing campaigns can become more sophisticated and effective over time, without requiring additional effort.

By utilizing AI to segment your email list, you can deliver more personalized emails to specific groups of people, resulting in better engagement and response rates.

➤ Tailor Email Retargeting

Using AI for email retargeting is a great way to reach customers with highly relevant emails. Did you know that 59% of consumers say emails impact their shopping decisions? Well, that was what Vidakovic (2023) of *text.cortex* discovered.

AI-powered tools like MailChimp can help eCommerce businesses by using predictive insights to target specific customers with relevant product offerings. The AI algorithms can also help in timing the delivery of targeted emails to ensure maximum impact.

With customized retargeting emails that include the right products, you can increase the chances of customers making a purchase and boost your sales.

➤ Check for errors in your email

Believe it or not, AI can proofread your emails really well! One popular tool is Grammarly, which does more than just check your work for spelling and grammar mistakes. It also analyzes your tone, clarity, and intent to help you communicate better.

Grammarly even has a browser extension that lets you check your work on most websites and web apps. How about if you don't have a Grammarly subscription? No worries! You can also use other AI tools like ChatGPT to proofread your emails and catch any mistakes before you hit send.

➢ Boost Your Sales with Product Recommendations

AI is a game-changer when offering tailored product recommendations to customers. It uses customer data to track their behavior on-site and then sends personalized emails with product suggestions. Businesses can use AI to make product recommendations based on customer interests and preferences.

For example, AI can analyze a customer's past purchases, browsing history, and shopping cart items to suggest products they are likely to be interested in. Moreover, AI can update emails in real-time to ensure that product recommendations are current and relevant.

When it comes to writing product descriptions, AI can help generate innovative and creative content for your products. You can use tools like Copy.ai or Textio to create compelling descriptions that capture the essence of your products. With AI, you can focus on making your products stand out, knowing that the language used to describe them is on point.

Monetizing your Audience

In today's era of big data, marketers need to use a range of tools to offer the ideal products and services for their intended audience at each stage of the customer journey. But how can businesses be certain that their marketing research and decisions are top-notch when converting data into ROI? The solution is simple: by utilizing AI.

Hines (2023) reported that Microsoft recently rolled out a new feature. It's called the ads for chat API, and it's designed to help businesses make money from their AI chat experiences without being intrusive.

The ads for chat API creates ads that are native to the chat experience and provides a win-win situation for all involved. Partners get to make money, consumers get a seamless chat experience, and advertisers get their message out there. Basically, businesses will make their money from the engagement of their audience. That's innovative of Microsoft.

Monetizing your audience can have many benefits beyond providing free resources. Offering digital products to your community can help bring people together, provide more value, and ultimately lead to greater satisfaction. By giving your audience a way to support your brand and invest in your offerings, you're creating a more enriching experience for everyone involved.

According to Lewis (2019), to make a profit without breaking the trust of your audience, it's essential to offer products they truly value. You've put in a lot of effort to establish a strong relationship with your followers, so it's vital to maintain that trust. In fact, by providing excellent products, you can even grow your following and show them why they should stick around.

According to the renowned Walt Disney, the creation of movies was not for the sole purpose of generating revenue, but instead, the revenue was utilized to produce more movies. This perspective can also be applied to monetizing your audience. The purpose of selling products is to strengthen your business and enable you to continue sharing your best ideas with the world.

You should consider these suggestions to monetize your audience:

1. Discover What Your Audience Craves

Chances are you have some idea about what your audience is interested in. Your content is likely what brought them together in the first place. But gaining more insights into your audience is always valuable, especially if you want to convert your free audience into potential customers for your products.

With AI, you can be more effective at discovering your audience's interest. And it can do it in several ways. For instance, AI tools can analyze customer data and behavior to identify patterns and preferences.

AI tools can also analyze social media activity and sentiment to understand better how customers perceive the business and its products. Additionally, AI can be used to conduct surveys and gather customer feedback, providing valuable insights into their wants and needs.

Finally, AI-powered chatbots can engage with customers in real-time, providing a personalized experience and helping you better understand your audience's needs and interests.

2. Craft a Winning Digital Product

Selling digital products is a great way to earn passive income, but if you want to maintain the trust of your followers, it's important to ensure you're offering something valuable. Here are some reasons why digital products are a smart business move:

- No financial investment in stock or product manufacturing.

- No logistical concerns about inventory, packaging, or shipping.

- Endless possibilities to create new products for any market or audience.

- Online delivery, with no risk of running out of stock.

- Budget-friendly, without shipping fees.

- High-profit margins with no recurring costs.

According to Susanna (2022) on *Shopify*, information products, in particular, are the most popular types of digital products people love to buy. User penetration of information products is expected to reach 15.9% by 2024.

To create a digital product that truly resonates with your audience, invest the time and energy to make it something you're proud of. People can tell when something was thrown together hastily. The objective is to develop products that are memorable and enduring, which in turn, strengthens the trust that your followers have in your brand.

One example of a successful digital product creator is Ashley Renee (Messy Eats Store), a keto food blogger and social media strategist. After her food videos went viral on TikTok, she started writing and selling keto cookbooks. Her high-demand recipes motivated her to self-publish, and now she can finance her lifestyle and teach others how to go viral on TikTok.

3. Make the First Sale

It's time to make that money! You've got your digital product and all the data you need; now it's time to sell it.

Here are some tips to help you out:

Start by offering something free, like a lite version of your paid course. This will give potential customers a taste of what you're offering and get them excited about buying.

Get people hyped up about your product by talking about it in the weeks leading up to launch. Share the benefits and explain why you made it – especially if it's because your audience asked for it.

Create a sense of urgency by offering limited-time promotions. For example, you could tell your followers that the first 75 users to buy your product get 50% off.

4. Avoid disappointing your followers with false promises

Maintaining the trust of your audience is key to building a successful online business. If you've established a loyal following that relies on you for free resources, you don't want to bait and switch them with sudden sales pitches.

The best way to avoid this is to continue providing value for free. In fact, veteran copywriter Bob Bly (cited by Lewis, 2019) recommends that at least 50% of the content you produce should be geared towards providing educational content for free. This means that as long as one half remains entertaining, value-packed, and free, it's okay for the other half to be geared toward selling your products.

Maintaining a clear and consistent brand voice across all your offerings is also important. You don't want your followers to feel like they've been tricked or misled, which can result in losing their trust. When promoting your digital products, ensure they align with your free resources. It should be clear to your audience that the same generous voice offering free advice also provides equally generous paid digital products.

Maintaining a balance between providing free and paid content helps to build a relationship of trust with your audience. It shows them that you're not just in it for the money but genuinely care about providing value and helping them achieve their goals. So, continue providing valuable resources for free and ensure that your paid digital products align with your brand and messaging.

5. Get Feedback and Expand Your Audience

Creating a valuable digital product is just the beginning of your journey. The real work begins after the launch. Your next goal should be to gather feedback from your customers to turn them into loyal fans. This step is crucial for building a trustworthy brand, but it can be nerve-wracking to hear criticism.

You might be scared to hear something like, "Your product wasn't worth the cost. I want my money back." But if you've created something valuable, this response is unlikely from most customers. Instead, you're likely to get a mix of insights about what people loved, hated, or didn't even notice about your product.

This feedback is gold. You can use it to improve your first product and create new ones your audience will enjoy. If everything goes well, you'll have fans who will buy anything you produce. These fans will buy your products and tell their friends about them.

As Kevin Kelly (cited by Lewis, 2019) points out, creating a high-tier fan base doesn't happen by accident. People get excited about ideas and products that add value to their lives. If you pay close attention to what your followers want and create top-notch products specifically for them, people will notice.

The key to success is to keep growing your audience by providing value, building trust, and engaging with them. If you keep doing this, you'll have a thriving business creating valuable products for paying fans who will stick with you for the long haul.

Using AI to Scale Your Online Business

This is the essence of this entire book. So, let's dig in to find out how AI can scale your business.

If you want to scale your online business, you should know

that AI can be a game-changer for you. You can use AI to identify new sales opportunities and personalize marketing campaigns to cater to your target audience. With AI, you can also provide faster and more accurate customer support, leading to increased customer satisfaction and loyalty.

But that's not all. AI can help you optimize your business operations, from creating content to managing your inventory. This optimization can lead to significant cost savings and increased efficiency, allowing you to focus on growing your business even more. So, if you're not already leveraging AI in your online business, it's time to start exploring its potential.

I'll highlight some cool ways to use AI tools to optimize your online business.

Here are the rewritten headings and paragraphs:

1. Automate Your Inventory Management

Tired of manually tracking inventory levels and restocking decisions? AI-powered machine learning algorithms can automate these processes for you. By predicting future demand and helping with restocking decisions, you'll have better inventory control, reduced stockouts, and lower carrying costs.

2. Provide 24/7 Customer Support with AI Chatbots

Nobody wants to wait for customer support, and with AI-powered chatbots, your customers won't have to. With 24/7 customer support, personalized interactions, and the ability to recommend products and answer frequently asked questions, chatbots can increase sales and customer satisfaction while freeing human representatives to handle more complex issues.

3. Prevent Fraud with AI Detection

E-commerce businesses are often targeted by fraud, but you can identify and prevent it with AI-powered machine learning algorithms. AI can help reduce chargebacks, protect your brand's reputation, and increase customer trust by analyzing customer data such as unusual purchasing patterns or shipping addresses.

4. Personalize Your Marketing Efforts with AI

Want to increase conversions and customer engagement? AI can help you create tailored marketing campaigns by analyzing customer data such as browsing history, purchase history, and social media activity. By personalizing your marketing efforts, you can stay ahead of the competition and maximize your profits.

5. Optimize Your Prices with AI-Powered Pricing

Stay ahead of the competition and maximize your profits with AI-powered price optimization. By analyzing vast amounts of data, including market trends, competitor prices, and customer behavior, AI can make pricing recommendations to help you optimize your pricing strategy.

6. Improve Your Supply Chain Efficiency with AI

AI can help you improve your supply chain's efficiency in various ways, from demand forecasting to logistics optimization. By automating processes and reducing lead times, you can improve delivery times and lower transportation costs, leading to improved customer satisfaction and increased profits.

Strategies to Increase Traffic and Engagement

Have you noticed how websites like Amazon, Netflix, and Google seem to know exactly what you like and show you content relevant to your interests? Well, it's all thanks to artificial intelligence. With technology evolving, more and more websites are now using AI to enhance their user experience and drive traffic to their site.

Want to drive more traffic to your website? I'm going to share three ways you can do it, and the best part is almost all of them are free.

Three ways to increase traffic and engagement on your website

Wait a moment. You don't have a website yet? Get one. Do you know why you need one? None of these strategies will make sense to you if you don't have a platform to implement them. Plus, your business stands a better chance of high visibility when you have a website.

1. Contents

2. SEO

3. Social media

Contents

Heads up! You must have content if you want to increase the number of visitors to your website. There's no way around it.

❖ **Starting a Business Blog**

Before you can start creating content, you'll need to set up your blog. Choose a platform that suits your needs, such as WordPress or Squarespace. Make sure to customize your blog's design and layout to reflect your brand.

❖ **Focus on evergreen topics**

While staying current with current events and trends is

important, creating content around evergreen topics will help your blog attract visitors over the long term. These types of posts are always relevant to your target audience and can continue to drive traffic to your site for years to come.

❖ Write irresistible headlines

Headlines are what grab readers' attention and entice them to click through to your content. Make sure to spend time crafting compelling headlines that accurately reflect your post's content.

❖ Invite guest bloggers

Having guest bloggers contribute to your blog can add diversity to your content and attract new readers. Encourage them to share their post with their audience and include links to your website.

❖ Use visuals

Incorporating visuals, such as images and videos, into your blog posts can make them more engaging and shareable. They can also help you rank higher in search results.

❖ Create a resource center

A dedicated page on your website for resources, such as eBooks, webinars, and templates, can keep visitors returning to your site. It's also a great way to showcase your expertise and build trust with your audience.

SEO

Ever heard of Search Engine Optimization (SEO)? It's all about making your website more visible in search results by optimizing it for search engines. It may appear complicated, but understanding the fundamentals can help you significantly improve your website's search engine rankings.

Target keywords to improve your website's search engine rankings. Here's how to do that.

1. Conduct keyword research using tools like Google Keyword Planner or SEMrush to identify which keywords are most relevant and have the highest search volume.

2. It's crucial to prioritize keywords with high search volume since they can drive traffic to your website better. To illustrate, let's say you're a blogger who wants to increase your website's visibility on search engines. Instead of targeting a specific phrase like "how to make homemade pasta" that only gets 20 searches per month, you could focus on a broader and more popular keyword such as "Italian cuisine" which receives over 5000 monthly searches. By targeting high-traffic keywords, you could attract more readers and increase your chances of converting them into loyal followers.

3. Incorporate your target keywords into your website's content in a natural and relevant way. This can include using them in headlines, meta descriptions, and throughout the body of your content. However, avoid keyword stuffing, as it can actually hurt your search engine rankings.

You can also use ***internal links*** to generate more traffic to your website. These links will lead them to other articles you've written on your blog site. Other benefits of these internal links are:

- It'll link to other pages on your site when you create and publish content.

- It'll keep visitors on your site longer, encouraging them to view more pages.

- You have the opportunity to provide more value to visitors, which can improve your site's ranking and drive more traffic.

You can also use ***backlinks***. When another website links to one of your pages using a specific word or phrase, it's called a backlink. And guess what? Search engines like Google view these links as "votes" for your page's relevance, quality, and authority. So the more relevant and high-quality backlinks you have, the higher your page will rank on search engine results pages.

Here are some ways to get more backlinks for your website:

- Reach out to bloggers or websites in your industry and offer to write a guest post for them. In return, include a link back to your own website in your author bio.

- Create high-quality, shareable content that other websites will want to link to.

- Participate in online communities and forums related to your industry and include a link to your website in your profile.

- List your website in relevant resource pages.

- Offer to exchange links with other websites in your industry, but make sure they have a good reputation and are relevant to your audience.

Social Media

I curated eight ways social media can generate traffic for your website from McCormick's (n.d) *WordStream* platform.

1. Promote your content on social: Share your content on social media channels that your audience loves. Twitter is perfect for short, catchy links, while Pinterest and Instagram are great for image posts. The more views you get, the more likely you are to get backlinks to your site.

2. Add hashtags: Use relevant hashtags on LinkedIn, Twitter, Instagram, and other social sites to increase your post's reach. Keep the hashtags specific to the post's topic, so the right people can find your content.

3. Target amplifiers: Create content for potential amplifiers, not just potential customers. These amplifiers include industry publications and external sources of influence like journalists and customer evangelists.

4. Post native LinkedIn articles: LinkedIn is a valuable publishing platform, so post content regularly. This can increase traffic to your site, visitors to your LinkedIn Company Page, and your reputation within your industry.

5. Interview industry thought leaders: You'd be surprised how many thought leaders will talk to you if you just ask. Interview them and publish the interviews on your blog. The name recognition will boost your credibility, and the interviewee will likely share the content too.

6. Add social share buttons: Make it easy for readers to share your content by adding social share buttons or the click-to-tweet feature to your site.

7. Research the competition: Use services like BuzzSumo to see what topics resonate with readers and make the rounds on social media. Emulate that kind of content to

bring traffic to your site.

8. Post at the right time: Use social media analytics to find the best times of day and week to share your blog post links. Start with the overall average best times and refine from there.

Case Studies of Successful Online Businesses

I've put together five case studies of successful online businesses that might inspire you:

1. Warby Parker

Warby Parker is an online eyewear retailer that disrupted the traditional eyewear industry with its affordable and stylish glasses. They started in 2010 with a simple concept: to sell prescription eyewear online. By using technology to create a better user experience, Warby Parker was able to offer high-quality, stylish glasses at a fraction of the cost of traditional eyewear retailers. They also introduced a "try-on-at-home" program, which allowed customers to test out glasses before making a purchase. Today, Warby Parker has over 100 retail stores and a loyal customer base valued at over $3 billion.

2. Airbnb

Airbnb is an online marketplace that connects travelers with local hosts who offer unique accommodations, from apartments to treehouses to castles. The company was founded in 2008 and has since grown into a global phenomenon, with over seven million listings in more than 220 countries. Airbnb's success is due in large part to its focus on creating a community-driven platform that encourages trust, safety, and authenticity. By building a platform that caters to both hosts and guests, Airbnb has created a thriving ecosystem of travelers and hosts alike.

3. Dollar Shave Club

Dollar Shave Club is an online subscription service that regularly delivers high-quality razors and grooming products to customers. The company was founded in 2011 with a simple mission: to provide affordable, high-quality razors to men. By leveraging the power of social media and viral marketing, Dollar Shave Club was able to quickly build a loyal customer base and disrupt the traditional razor industry. In 2016, Dollar Shave Club was acquired by Unilever for a reported $1 billion.

4. Glossier

Glossier is an online beauty brand that creates simple, effective skincare and makeup products catering to a younger, more socially engaged demographic. Founded in 2014 by Emily Weiss, the brand has grown into a cult favorite, with a loyal following of millennials and Gen Zers. Glossier's success is mainly due to its focus on community building and user-generated content. By encouraging their customers to share their Glossier experiences on social media, the brand has built a powerful online community that drives word-of-mouth marketing and brand awareness.

5. Peloton

Peloton is an online fitness company that offers high-quality workout equipment and live-streaming fitness classes to customers around the world. The company was founded in 2012 with a simple mission: to bring the boutique fitness studio experience to people's homes. By combining technology, community, and high-quality fitness equipment, Peloton has created a loyal following of customers willing to pay a premium for their services. Peloton has over four million members, a thriving online community, and a market cap of over $30 billion.

Chapter Recap

This chapter covers key topics related to creating a growth strategy for your online business with the help of AI. It explores developing an effective sales funnel, building an email list, and monetizing your audience. It also provides insights into using AI to scale your business and increase traffic and engagement. The chapter concludes with real-life case studies of successful online businesses implementing these strategies to achieve remarkable growth and success.

Chapter Seven

Marketing Strategies

What really decides consumers to buy or not to buy is the content of your advertising, not its form.
—David Ogilvy

I stumbled on a magazine some years ago where I read about a young entrepreneur who wanted to sell his homemade cookies online. He spent weeks baking the perfect recipe and was excited to start his business. But when he launched his website, he quickly realized that no one was buying his cookies.

Feeling discouraged, the young entrepreneur decided to seek advice from an experienced expert in marketing. The marketer told him, "Marketing is like fishing. You have to know what bait to use and where to cast your line."

The young entrepreneur took this advice to heart and started experimenting with different marketing strategies. He tried social media ads, email marketing, and even influencer collaborations. But nothing seemed to work.

The young entrepreneur didn't stop trying until an idea lit up in his head. He decided to offer a free sample of his cookies to anyone who signed up for his email list. People started signing up left and right, and soon the young entrepreneur had a growing list of email subscribers.

He then sent out a special email offer to his list, offering a discount on his cookies for a limited time. Sales started pouring in, and his business began to take off.

From that day forward, the young entrepreneur learned that marketing was all about experimentation and finding the right strategy for your business. And just like fishing, sometimes you have to be patient and keep trying until you catch the big one.

There's no one-fit marketing strategy. However, there are basic principles guiding marketing. You've got to pay attention to the strategies I'll share here and come up with something that works for you.

Sales and Marketing

When considering running a successful business, it is crucial to pay attention to these two major components: sales and marketing. These two elements work cohesively with the ultimate aim of acquiring and retaining customers for a company.

Although sales and marketing share a common objective, their approaches differ. When it comes to a business, marketing is all about spreading the word about a brand or organization, while sales take that hype and turn it into cash by getting people to buy things. It's like marketing is the cool party promoter, and sales is the guy selling the tickets at the door. Is that simple enough?

Let's look at areas where they differ:

- Process

- Goals

- Strategies

- Prospects

Process

According to Casarella (2021), when it comes to getting your brand and product out there, you subscribe to the marketing process. Marketing is about making your product or service known to new customers or reminding former ones. To do this, businesses must clearly explain what they're offering, how it solves customer problems, and how much it costs. Then the marketing team needs to determine who's most likely to be interested and where to find them.

Now, sales is a whole different ball game. The sales team's main goal is to turn people who have heard of the brand into paying customers so the company can make some money. They talk to customers and give them the info they need to decide whether to buy the product or service. To make it happen, the sales team has a plan outlining their actions, resources, and goals.

Goals

The main goal of a business's marketing is to get the word out about its product, company, or brand through clear and effective communication. The idea is to show the big picture and explain how the product or service benefits as many people as possible, leading to more potential customers.

Now, regarding sales, things are a bit more short-term. The sales team's goals are based on quotas and volume and are usually set for a few months or a quarter. The team must sell enough to generate the profits necessary to keep the business running. That's why they have specific goals and targets to meet.

Strategies

To market a product or service effectively, the marketing team must gather information about its target audience. This allows them to test out various strategies and determine what works and what doesn't. Popular forms of marketing strategies include online marketing, print marketing, blog marketing, and focus groups.

Sales strategies, on the other hand, involve connecting with potential customers, understanding their needs, and ultimately converting them into paying customers. A salesperson typically initiates contact through a phone call, networking event, or online platform. Depending on the scope of the product or service, the salesperson will then pitch it to the customer in hopes of closing the sale.

Prospects

Regarding marketing versus sales, the potential audience for marketing is typically larger. The marketing team's main goal is to identify and target a specific audience while creating brand awareness. Their primary focus is on generating new leads and building their customer base.

On the other hand, the sales team is more focused on leveraging existing relationships and connections with known prospects and current clients. Their primary objective is to convert these individuals into paying customers and maintain their loyalty to the brand.

But there has to be a meeting point between these two. Let's see:

Regarding sales and marketing, their goals may differ, but they do have a lot of overlap. That's why it's important for these two departments to work together and align their interests. They can achieve greater success by forming a partnership and sharing any overlapping materials.

For larger companies, creating a service-level agreement (SLA) can be a great way to build partnerships between teams. This agreement outlines a set of deliverables that one department agrees to provide to the other, which can help clarify expectations and ensure everyone is on the same page.

An SLA may not be necessary for smaller businesses, but management should still make it clear to both teams what their positions are in the market. The marketing team should inform the sales team when they are running campaigns so the sales team can maximize their efforts during those times.

Similarly, the sales team should share customer data with the marketing team. This can provide valuable insights into the target audience's demographics and which efforts have been successful, allowing the marketing team to refine their strategies accordingly.

AI as an Effective Marketing Tool

Doyle (2023) rightly observed that in today's fast-paced business environment, marketing teams are always searching for new and creative ways to reach their target audience and achieve their objectives. But with limited resources, it can be challenging to keep up with the demand for results. That's why many organizations are turning to artificial intelligence platforms as a solution.

AI marketing platforms help alleviate workload and provide a more comprehensive understanding of a company's customer base. With data-driven insights, companies can develop more effective strategies that lead to higher conversion rates. It's no wonder that more and more businesses are adopting this technology to achieve their marketing goals.

So, let's just call this type of marketing-powered-AI AI marketing. Now let's try to give it a proper definition.

So, what would you say AI marketing is? Give it a try.

Basically, AI marketing is incorporating conversational AI tools into marketing efforts. And I tell you what, that is a game changer in the business world. These tools can assess current strategies' success and generate new marketing ideas and content. By utilizing these tools, companies can take their marketing efforts to the next level and stay ahead of the competition.

AI is like the new kid on the block in digital marketing. It's especially useful when speed is of the essence. Basically, AI marketing tools collect data about customers and use that information to learn how to talk to them in the best way possible. Then they can send personalized messages to customers at the perfect time without needing anyone on the marketing team to push a button.

I believe those tools are super-efficient. And that just made business more interesting. Nowadays, many digital marketers use AI to boost their team or handle more straightforward tasks that don't need a lot of human touch.

What are the benefits of AI marketing?

❖ **Get More Done in Less Time**

One of the biggest advantages of using AI in marketing is that it saves time. By streamlining the content creation process, AI tools allow businesses to focus on other important tasks that require human attention.

❖ **Make Better Decisions with Data**

AI-powered marketing tools are equipped to provide businesses with detailed insights and data-driven recommendations. This helps businesses make more informed decisions about their marketing spend, leading to better results and a higher ROI.

❖ **Spark Creativity and Generate Ideas**

With AI content generators, like Jasper, businesses can easily generate new marketing ideas and content. These tools offer the benefit of being your brainstorming buddy, helping to kickstart your imagination and inspire creativity.

❖ **Enhance Collaboration Among Teams**

AI content tools provide a central hub for team collaboration, enabling all members to work together on marketing assets that match the same style and tone of voice. This creates a more cohesive brand identity and improves cross-collaboration among teams.

Examples of AI Marketing Tools

ChatGPT

This particular AI tool is the talk of the town. And it's been making heads turn in different institutions. It's been causing a lot of revolution out there. That's why I made it the focal point of this book.

As an AI language model, ChatGPT can be a powerful

marketing tool for businesses looking to engage with their customers more personalized and conversationally. With its ability to generate human-like responses and carry on conversations, ChatGPT can be used for various marketing purposes, such as customer support, lead generation, and content creation.

One way to leverage ChatGPT for marketing is by creating chatbots that can interact with customers in real time, answering their questions and providing support. Chatbots powered by ChatGPT can be trained to understand natural language queries, making them more effective at handling complex inquiries.

Another way to use ChatGPT for marketing is to generate content, such as blog posts or social media updates. By inputting a few keywords or prompts, ChatGPT can generate unique and engaging content to share with audiences.

Grammarly

For anyone who writes, Grammarly is a game-changer. This AI-powered tool is more than just a spelling and grammar checker; it can help with tone, readability, and engagement, making it an essential tool for marketing materials. And it's not just for word processing software; it works with most content management systems (CMS) and web browsers. Plus, Grammarly has big plans to add even more features, including ideation tools that can help you generate new concepts and ideas.

AISEO.ai

Have you ever written a blog post and thought, "This would make a great tweet or YouTube video too"? AISEO has got you covered with its content repurposing tool. This free AI tool can transform your existing content into a new format, whether it's a social media campaign or an email newsletter. Another AISEO tool worth mentioning is the paraphraser, which can tweak your content with AI, making it more engaging and appropriate for different audiences.

Jasper.ai

If you're ever stuck for inspiration, Jasper.ai is here to help. This AI-powered tool is great for creating new and fresh marketing content. All you need to do is feed it a few prompts, and it will generate a range of options for you. Over time, the system "learns" your preferences, making the content creation process even more personalized. Jasper.ai can even generate art from existing marketing materials, offering new ways to use old content.

Growthbar

If you're looking to boost your website's SEO, then Growthbar is your tool. Unlike other SEO tools that give you feedback after the fact, Growthbar provides real-time feedback and suggestions directly in your browser. It can even analyze your existing content to see where you can improve it and suggest internal links to promote your content and services. And if you have an older website with legacy content.

Smartwriter.ai

Personalization is key when it comes to marketing, and Smartwriter.ai is an AI tool that can help you achieve it effortlessly. This tool is especially useful for creating personalized emails, whether it's a cold call or a letter to existing customers. With its deep enrichment feature, Smartwriter.ai can research leads and modify templates to fit the tone and style of your target audience. Say goodbye to generic emails and hello to personalized ones that will grab your audience's attention.

Smartly.io

Making changes to your marketing strategy can be risky, but it's also necessary to stay ahead of the game. That's where Smartly.io comes in handy. This campaign manager uses AI to create and evaluate A/B/C tests and other variants to see which ones perform the best. The AI-driven feedback helps businesses make informed decisions on how to optimize their campaigns for a better ROI.

Tips and Tricks for Effective Marketing

The tips I'll supply here are primarily what you can do with ChatGPT to enhance your marketing. I assure you, this tool is so loaded with data that it churns out information in seconds. That makes the job easier for you. Why go through the stress of scouring the net for information when there's an efficient assistant?

Here are 13 tricks for using ChatGPT for effective marketing:

1. **Generate copy for your marketing assets:** You can use ChatGPT to generate ad copy for a new product, write social media captions for an upcoming campaign, or even draft an outline for a blog post.

2. **Ask ChatGPT for Keyword Research:** You can ask ChatGPT to recommend keywords related to your product or service, and it can also help you identify the search intent behind each keyword, which will help you write relevant content.

3. **Get marketing tool recommendations:** You can ask ChatGPT for recommendations on marketing tools, such as the best social media management software, SEO tools, or email marketing platforms.

4. **Lead generation:** ChatGPT can be used to build chatbots that engage with site visitors and gather information for

lead generation purposes. Marketers can also use ChatGPT to engage with website visitors and gather valuable segmentation information.

5. **Content ideation:** You can ask ChatGPT for post ideas based on topics or existing content, use it to research a topic, curate the top articles on a topic, or have it simplify a complex concept for you so you can simplify it for your readers.

6. **Learn shortcuts and formulas:** You can ask ChatGPT for spreadsheet formulas, regular expressions, and other strings that are evergreen and can help you with data processing and analysis.

7. **Ask ChatGPT for Topic Clusters:** You can ask ChatGPT to organize a list of keywords into content clusters to help you create an effective pillar page outline. For example, if you're an SEO agency, you could ask ChatGPT to organize a list of keywords related to your agency, the specific industries you work with, the services you provide, and your level of expertise.

8. **Writing Assistance:** ChatGPT can assist you with various writing tasks, such as generating topic ideas, outlining articles, and even writing full articles. For example, if you're a blogger stuck on what to write about next, you can ask ChatGPT for ideas on a particular topic,

and it can provide you with a list of suggestions.

9. **Language Translation:** ChatGPT can help with language translation for various languages. For instance, if you're working on a document that needs translating into Spanish, you can ask ChatGPT to translate it for you.

10. **Learning Assistance:** ChatGPT can help with learning tasks, such as answering questions about a particular subject or explaining complex topics. For example, if you're a student studying for an exam, you can ask ChatGPT to explain a difficult concept, and it can provide you with a clear and concise explanation.

11. **Research Assistance:** ChatGPT can help with research tasks, such as finding relevant information on a particular topic or providing sources for research papers. For instance, if you're working on a research paper and need to find sources to support your argument, you can ask ChatGPT to provide you with a list of relevant sources.

12. **Task Automation:** ChatGPT can automate various tasks, such as sending emails, scheduling appointments, and even ordering food. For example, if you're a busy professional and don't have time to schedule appointments, you can ask ChatGPT to do it.

13. **Data Analysis:** ChatGPT can help with data analysis

tasks, such as providing insights into customer behavior or identifying trends in data. For instance, if you're a business owner and want to analyze customer feedback to improve your products or services, you can ask ChatGPT to provide insights based on the data.

Automate Your Marketing Strategy

Let's go over this again. You can use ChatGPT to automate your marketing strategy in the following ways:

1. Content Creation

One of the most time-consuming aspects of marketing is creating high-quality content that resonates with your audience. ChatGPT can assist with this by generating content ideas, headlines, and even full-length articles based on your desired topic and keywords. This can save you valuable time and effort while ensuring your content is optimized for search engines and tailored to your target audience.

2. Lead Generation

Chatbots are a powerful tool for generating leads, as they can interact with potential customers in real time and collect their contact information. ChatGPT can help you build a chatbot that's personalized to your brand and can answer common questions from prospects and direct them to the appropriate resources. With ChatGPT, you can create a conversational flow that encourages engagement and prompts users to take action.

3. Customer Support

Providing excellent customer support is crucial for building brand loyalty and retention. With ChatGPT, you can automate your customer support process by creating a chatbot that can answer frequently asked questions, provide troubleshooting assistance, and even handle basic tasks like account management. By using ChatGPT to streamline your customer support, you can free up your team's time to focus on more complex issues and improve the overall customer experience.

4. Social Media Management

ChatGPT can be a valuable tool for automating social media management, from scheduling posts to analyzing audience data. With ChatGPT, you can optimize your posting schedule based on peak usage times and audience behavior and analyze data to gain insights into consumer behavior and preferences. Additionally, ChatGPT can recommend the best ad formats and creative elements for your campaigns based on data analysis.

5. Customer Surveys

Getting to know your target audience is crucial for creating effective marketing strategies, and customer surveys are an effective way to collect feedback and insights. ChatGPT can help you generate customer surveys tailored to your specific business and audience and provide valuable insights into customer behavior, preferences, and pain points.

6. Chatbot Ideas

Adding a chatbot to your website can effectively generate leads, engage with customers, and collect feedback. ChatGPT can provide you with ideas for chatbot prompts and answers tailored to your brand and audience, ensuring that your chatbot is engaging and effective.

Optimizing Sales with AI

As the sales industry becomes increasingly competitive, sales teams must explore new ways to optimize their approach to win more deals. Artificial intelligence (AI) presents a compelling opportunity to improve sales operations and drive revenue growth. In this note, we'll explore how to optimize sales with AI and explain each point in detail.

Leverage AI for lead scoring and prioritization: Sales teams can use AI-powered lead scoring and prioritization tools to identify the most qualified leads in their pipeline quickly. By analyzing data such as a lead's job title, company size, and engagement history, these tools can provide a score that indicates the likelihood of that lead converting into a customer. This allows sales reps to focus their efforts on the leads that are most likely to close, improving their efficiency and increasing their chances of success (Sood, 2020).

Use AI to personalize outreach: Personalized outreach is essential for sales success, but it can be time-consuming to create tailored messages for each prospect. AI-powered sales tools can help automate this process by analyzing data such as a prospect's interests, engagement history, and communication preferences to generate personalized messages. This can help sales reps save time while also increasing the effectiveness of their outreach (Gartner, 2020).

Leverage AI for sales forecasting: Sales forecasting is a critical aspect of sales operations, but it can be challenging to predict revenue accurately. AI-powered forecasting tools can help improve accuracy by analyzing historical data, market trends, and other factors impacting sales performance. This can help sales teams better plan their resources and set realistic targets (Nagarajan, 2021).

Use AI to automate administrative tasks: Sales reps spend a significant amount of time on administrative tasks, such as data entry, scheduling, and reporting. AI-powered tools can automate these tasks, allowing reps to spend more time selling. This can help improve their productivity and job satisfaction while also reducing the risk of errors (Kissmetrics, 2021).

Leverage AI for competitive intelligence: Competitive intelligence can provide valuable insights into a company's competitors, market trends, and customer needs. AI-powered tools can help sales teams quickly gather and analyze this information, providing actionable insights to inform sales strategy and tactics. This can help sales teams stay ahead of the competition and win more deals (Meltwater, 2021).

Sales Automation with AI

By leveraging the power of AI, you can automate repetitive tasks, streamline workflows, and improve overall efficiency. In this final section of this chapter, we'll explore how you can use AI to automate your sales process and achieve better results.

Lead Scoring

One of the most important aspects of sales is identifying qualified leads. AI can help with this process by scoring leads based on various criteria such as demographics, behavior, and engagement. By using machine learning algorithms to analyze and prioritize leads, your sales team can focus their efforts on the leads most likely to convert, saving time and improving conversion rates. (Baker, 2021)

Sales Forecasting

Predicting sales is essential for effective resource allocation and planning. AI can help by analyzing past sales data and identifying trends and patterns to generate accurate sales forecasts. By automating this process, you can free up your sales team's time to focus on more strategic tasks. (Columbus, 2020)

Personalization

Personalization is key to effective sales. AI can help by analyzing data on customer behavior and preferences to provide personalized recommendations and content. By delivering targeted messaging and content, you can improve customer engagement and drive conversions. (Baker, 2021)

Chatbots

Chatbots can be a powerful tool for automating customer interactions and driving sales. Using AI-powered chatbots, you can provide customers with personalized support and assistance 24/7. Chatbots can help answer frequently asked questions, guide customers through the buying process, and even provide recommendations based on customer preferences. (Columbus, 2020)

Sales Performance Analytics

AI can help you measure the effectiveness of your sales

process by providing insights into key performance metrics such as conversion rates, customer retention, and revenue growth. By analyzing this data, you can identify areas for improvement and adjust your sales strategy accordingly. (Baker, 2021)

Chapter Recap

The chapter explores the intersection of sales, marketing, and artificial intelligence (AI). It highlights how AI can be used as an effective marketing tool and offers tips and tricks for effective marketing. The chapter then delves into automating marketing strategies, discussing how AI can be used to streamline marketing processes and increase efficiency.

The chapter also covers optimizing sales with AI, discussing how AI-powered sales tools can enhance sales processes and drive revenue growth. Additionally, it highlights the benefits of sales automation with AI, offering insights into how AI can be used to automate sales processes and reduce manual labor.

Overall, the chapter provides a comprehensive overview of the role of AI in sales and marketing and highlights the various ways AI can be used to improve business operations and drive growth.

Chapter Eight

Troubleshooting and Problem-Solving

The real question is, when will we draft an artificial intelligence bill of rights? What will that consist of? And who will get to decide that?
– Gray Scott

While AI can be a powerful tool for optimizing operations and identifying problems, it is not a perfect solution. Business owners and decision-makers must learn to use AI critically and supplement it with their own judgment and intuition.

It reminds me of a small business owner who ran a successful coffee shop in my ever-bustling city. Although he was doing fine with his startup, he was always looking for ways to improve it.

So, one of those days, he noticed that his sales had been

decreasing gradually, and he couldn't quite figure out why. He tried different marketing strategies, including changing his menu and even running promotions, but nothing seemed to work.

That's when he turned to AI for help. He invested in a sophisticated AI program that promised to help him analyze his business data and optimize his operations. At first, the AI seemed to work wonders. It identified the root cause of the business owner's sales decline and suggested a range of solutions. The young business owner was thrilled and quickly implemented the recommended changes.

However, as time went on, he noticed that the AI was not as perfect as he had initially thought. It sometimes misinterpreted data or failed to consider certain variables, leading to inaccurate recommendations. Soon, he realized that AI was not a perfect solution to his business problems. He needed to use his own judgment and intuition to make the final call.

That doesn't mean he discarded the AI tool entirely, rather, he used it to supplement his decision-making process. He learned to interpret the AI's recommendations critically and make adjustments accordingly. That saved his business and got it booming again.

As this book reaches its final chapter, I must emphasize that AI technology will continue to advance and undoubtedly play an increasingly important role in business operations. However, it is important to remember that AI is not a replacement for human intelligence and intuition but rather a tool to supplement and enhance them.

Dealing with Changes in the AI Market

Attarbashi (n.d), CEO of AI Bees, observed that similar to past human inventions like the steam engine, electricity, and the internet, any new innovation that brings value, regardless of initial concerns or fears, tends to have a beneficial effect on society as a whole.

Undoubtedly, many people have been nursing the fear of being retrenched now that AIs can do virtually everything and anything humans claim to be monotonous. But as Attarbashi observed, AIs are tools to make a living and working easier for humans. To see AI as a threat to humans is an indication that we know nearly nothing about AI.

In fact, we are living in a time of constant change, where industries are being revolutionized, and new players are entering the market. The concept of monopoly is becoming obsolete, and smaller companies can now compete and thrive in the marketplace by implementing the right strategies and innovative products. Thanks to AI.

To adequately deal with the changes AI is causing in the industry, you need to know what AI is doing in the real sense.

What changes is AI making in the business industry?

Market and Customer Insights

AI can be used to analyze market and customer data. This information can be obtained from a variety of sources, including social media, the web, and system matrices. Predictive analysis can identify patterns in the data that can be used to develop better products and services. AI-based systems can optimize marketing strategies, helping businesses reduce marketing expenses while increasing the effectiveness of marketing campaigns.

Virtual Assistance

Chatbots and virtual assistants are becoming increasingly popular as they can provide customers with quick and efficient service. Chatbots can answer simple queries, freeing up human agents to tackle more complex issues. Virtual assistants can interact with customers, helping businesses engage with them more personally. AI-driven applications can automate business processes, making them more agile.

Data Unlocking

With the rise of unstructured data, analyzing this data is becoming increasingly important. AI can analyze vast amounts of data and identify patterns to develop better products and services. By analyzing customer conversations, businesses can identify their personality types and offer them compatible services.

Efficient Sales Process

Sales processes are becoming more efficient, thanks to AI. E-commerce companies are using AI to customize products based on the buyer's preferences, increasing the chances of conversion. AI can develop a sales pitch that reaches the right customer at the right time on the right platform.

Personalized Customer Experience

AI can be used to provide a more personalized experience for customers. By analyzing vast amounts of data, AI can identify patterns in a customer's behavior, allowing businesses to engage with them more personally. This can lead to increased customer engagement and loyalty.

The team at Apogaeis (n.d) admitted that AI is not a disruptor but rather an enabler. It offers many benefits to businesses, from enhancing customer service to improving the efficiency of business processes. As such, businesses should embrace AI as part of their overall strategy.

After conducting a survey on AI and the revolution it's causing, the Accenture Institute for High Performance claimed that by 2035, artificial intelligence could double the annual economic growth rates of many developed countries. Sounds good, right?

In the US alone, the annual growth rate could go up by 2%, which would mean an extra $8.3 trillion with AI adoption. And in the UK, AI could add an additional $814 billion to the economy, increasing the annual growth rate from 2.5% to 3.9%.

It's pretty clear that we're already seeing a massive tech-driven transformation happening in the business world, and it's helping us overcome all sorts of obstacles to achieve optimal growth.

Back to that question, "How do I deal with this?"

The best way is to be optimistic and leverage everything that AI offers. Jettison your fears. AI won't take your job or one day turn against you in your side hustle. It's a tool created to help you.

Managing Cash Flow, Budget, and Financial Risks

The International Monetary Fund (IMF) agrees with Mirestean et al. (2021) that the financial sector is being transformed by the ability to gather vast amounts of data from the environment and use artificial intelligence and machine learning (ML) to process it.

This technology is helping to predict economic, financial, and risk events with greater accuracy. It's also changing financial markets and making risk management and compliance more effective. Plus, central banks can use new tools to achieve their monetary and macroprudential goals thanks to AI/ML.

It's essential to keep track of the money that flows in and out of your business every day. Failing to do so can lead to financial troubles, and you might not have enough money to pay your bills. This is what we call cash flow risk, which means you're at risk of running out of cash.

The good news is that if you're looking to manage your business's cash flow better, some useful tools can make the process a whole lot easier. By leveraging AI technology, you can automate many cash flow-related tasks, analyze data in real time, predict trends, and gain valuable insights to help you make better decisions.

Tips for Managing Your Cash Flow

Managing cash flow can be difficult, but it is necessary to keep your business running smoothly. Luckily, some best practices can help you minimize cash flow risk and optimize your financial performance.

1. Invest in Automation and AI

One of the best ways to reduce financial risk is to have complete visibility and control over your company's financial activity. One tool that can be utilized to mitigate financial risk is "Xero," an accounting software that offers features like real-time cash flow management, automated invoicing, and payment reminders. By using Xero, you can gain insight into your business's financial health and take necessary measures to reduce financial risk.

For example, if you're a small business owner, you can use Xero to keep track of your expenses, generate reports, and forecast cash flow. With this information, you can identify potential financial risks, such as late payments or unexpected expenses, and take action to minimize their impact.

Additionally, Xero can help you automate routine tasks like invoicing and payment processing, reducing the risk of human error and improving the accuracy of your financial data. By utilizing Xero, you can effectively manage your cash flow, reduce financial risk, and make informed financial decisions.

2. Optimize Your Cash Inflow

Maximizing your incoming cash flows is essential to ensuring business continuity and growth. You can achieve this by offering customers various payment options, promptly issuing and following up on invoices, providing incentives for early payment, and selling unpaid invoices. You can also expand your customer base by developing new goods or services, marketing to new markets, and offering a referral program.

3. Optimize Your Outgoing Cash Flows

To get the biggest ROI for your expenses, you need to eliminate unnecessary costs, make strategic upgrades to equipment and technology, optimize your workflows, and negotiate the best possible payment terms with vendors. Automating your procure-to-pay process can help you achieve all this more efficiently while also reducing rogue spending and invoice fraud.

Let's also talk about budget forecasting. It is crucial to your business's cash flow.

So, what is budget forecasting?

Schunemann (n.d.) says that budget forecasting is the process of estimating your future income and expenses. It's like taking a peek into your financial future to see how much money you'll have and how much you'll need to spend.

The main goal of budget forecasting is to get an idea of your financial position at a specific time, using the budget for the upcoming period as one of your data sources. This way, you can predict whether your company will have enough money to cover all its bills and debts and how much profit it could make.

Budget forecasting is done to simulate what will happen when you create a budget and set expectations for the following year. It helps you predict how much money you'll have left after all your expenses and how much you can save or invest. With a solid budget forecast, you can confidently plan and make decisions, knowing that you have a good idea of what to expect in the future.

In short, forecasting your budget is an essential step for any business because it allows you to anticipate future expenses, revenues, and cash flows.

But traditional methods for budget forecasting can be tedious and prone to human errors. Hence, businesses increasingly seek artificial intelligence (AI) to improve their budget forecasting capabilities. AI has the potential to automate and optimize the budget forecasting process, but it also has its own set of challenges and limitations.

AI in Budget Forecasting

According to Weksler (n.d), AI can be utilized for budget forecasting by utilizing complex algorithms and advanced data analysis techniques to create, evaluate, and adjust budget forecasts. With AI's ability to analyze historical data, market conditions, current trends, and external factors, it can generate more realistic and precise budget forecasts.

Additionally, AI can recognize potential risks and opportunities, learn from feedback, and enhance its performance over time, making it more adaptable and capable of responding to changes in various situations.

- AI can save time and resources for budget forecasting.

- AI can improve accuracy and reliability in budget forecasting.

- AI can automate and streamline the budget forecasting process.

- AI can handle large, complex data sets and provide faster and more frequent updates.

- AI can reduce human errors and biases and provide more consistent and objective budget forecasts.

- AI can account for uncertainty and volatility and provide a range of possible outcomes and probabilities.

- AI can provide insights and recommendations for budget forecasting.

- AI can identify key drivers, trends, and patterns and suggest optimal actions and alternatives.

- AI can enable scenario planning and simulation and help to evaluate the impact and trade-offs of different budget decisions.

Addressing Customers' Complaints and Negative Feedback

According to Phillips (2022), the phrase "the customer is always right," coined by Harry Gordon Selfridge more than a century ago, is no longer adequate in the current business landscape, where customer expectations and regulations have evolved. In today's highly competitive market, companies need to ensure that their customer service processes are efficient and reliable or risk facing significant penalties, damage to their reputation, and customer churn. As a result, many organizations are turning to artificial intelligence (AI) and analytics technology to improve their complaint management processes.

AI-powered complaint management offers a range of benefits for companies, including the ability to proactively identify, classify, report, and remediate complaints. According to a study by PwC, approximately 86% of business leaders consider AI a mainstream technology, and it is increasingly being used for complaint management.

By providing a comprehensive view of complaints, AI can help companies comply with regulations while also gaining a better understanding of the impact of complaints on their organization. Companies need to be able to identify, remediate, and prevent complaints effectively to improve their complaint management processes.

AI can help organizations automate complaint management processes, such as identifying and classifying complaints across all channels and tracking remediation workflows. Additionally, AI can provide insights into the root causes of complaints and offer proactive analytics that help organizations reduce future complaints.

Rahal (2021) stated that online reviews can heavily impact your business's success. In fact, research shows that 93% of customers are influenced by online reviews when making purchasing decisions. Therefore, it is crucial to handle customer complaints effectively to avoid missing out on potential sales.

Avoiding Burnout and Maintaining Motivation

Have you ever felt so stressed out that it affected your mental and physical health? That's what we call burnout, which is a medical disorder that happens when you experience excessive and prolonged stress.

Back in the 1970s, psychologist Herbert Freudenberger coined the term, and since then, Professor Christina Maslach has been one of the foremost researchers on the topic.

Although we often hear the word "burnout" these days, it's not just a buzzword. It can lead to severe mental and physical health issues, as was the case for Arianna Huffington, who suffered from exhaustion and burnout just two years after creating The Huffington Post, which resulted in her collapsing and requiring four stitches in her right eye.

According to Knight (2015), it's not uncommon to feel burned out at work, even if you're passionate about your job. You might feel drained after completing a major project and struggle to find motivation for the next one.

Tips on How to Avoid Burnouts and Stay motivated

Take Breaks

It can be tempting to work for hours on end without taking a break, especially when you're a businessperson and every minute counts. However, taking regular breaks is crucial for maintaining productivity and preventing burnout. When you work for an extended time without taking a break, your brain becomes exhausted, and your performance suffers.

To avoid this, schedule regular breaks throughout your day. This could mean getting up from your desk and going for a walk, doing some stretches, or just taking a few deep breaths. Setting a reminder on your phone or computer can help you remember to take breaks when you need them.

Establish Priorities

As a business person, it's easy to get overwhelmed by the sheer number of tasks on your to-do list. When everything feels urgent, it can be hard to know where to start. That's why it's important to establish priorities. Take time to reflect on your goals and determine what tasks are most important to achieving them. You might find it helpful to create a roadmap or action plan that breaks down your goals into smaller, more manageable tasks. This will help you stay focused and avoid getting sidetracked by less important tasks.

Set Goals

Setting goals is a powerful way to stay motivated and focused on what's important. When you have a clear idea of what you want to achieve, staying on track and avoiding distractions is easier. Setting short-term goals can be especially helpful, as they give you a sense of progress and accomplishment along the way.

Whether it's a project deadline or a personal milestone, setting goals can help you stay motivated and productive. Just make sure your goals are realistic and achievable so you don't end up feeling discouraged or overwhelmed. Remember to celebrate your successes along the way, no matter how small they may seem.

Take Care of Your Health

As a business person, it's easy to get caught up in your work and neglect your health. But the truth is, your health is crucial to your success. If you're not taking care of yourself, you're likely to experience burnout and other health issues that can impact your business. That's why it's important to make time for self-care.

This could mean getting enough sleep, eating a balanced diet, staying hydrated, and exercising regularly. It's also important to take care of your mental health, whether that means practicing mindfulness or seeking support from a therapist. Remember, taking care of yourself is not selfish – it's essential for your success.

Connect with Others

Entrepreneurship can be a lonely journey, but it doesn't have to be. Connecting with other businesspersons and like-minded individuals can provide valuable support and encouragement along the way. Consider joining a local business group, networking organization, or attending industry events and conferences. Online communities can also be a great way to connect with others in your field. Don't be afraid to reach out and make new connections – you never know where they might lead.

Find a Work-Life Balance

Finally, it's important to find a balance between your work and personal life. When you're a businessperson, it can be tempting to work all the time, but this can lead to burnout and other health issues. Finding a work-life balance that works for you is essential for your overall well-being. This could mean setting specific work hours and sticking to them or taking breaks throughout the day to focus on personal activities.

It's also important to take time off when you need it, whether that means a vacation or a mental health day. Remember, you're not just a businessperson – you're a whole person, and taking care of all aspects of your life is important.

According to Buffini (2022), recognizing the warning signs of burnout is crucial in preventing it from taking a toll on your well-being and work. It can slowly manifest itself in various ways, affecting your productivity, motivation, and overall mental and physical health. Therefore, it's important to take heed of these signs before it's too late.

If you find yourself constantly feeling drained and depleted, it's time to take a step back and assess your situation. Ignoring the symptoms and pushing yourself beyond your limits can have serious consequences. Take the time to evaluate your daily routine, workload, and lifestyle habits to identify areas that may be contributing to your burnout.

Remember, taking care of yourself is crucial for your personal well-being and your business's success. Neglecting your needs and overworking yourself can lead to decreased productivity, motivation, and overall performance. Prioritizing self-care practices such as exercise, meditation, and healthy eating habits can help you avoid burnout and keep you on track toward achieving your goals.

Dealing with Legal and Regulatory Issues

As AI continues to advance, it raises new and important legal and ethical questions. Some have suggested the need for AI ethicists to help navigate this technological advance.

Ethical and legal issues have been highlighted by various

organizations around the world, such as the British House of Commons and the European Commission's High-Level Expert Group on Artificial Intelligence ("AI HLEG"). Trustworthy AI is one of the main requirements that the ethical guidelines suggest. It should have an ethical purpose and be technically robust and reliable to prevent unintentional harm.

In Canada, the Treasury Board Secretariat of Canada is looking at issues around the responsible use of AI in government programs and services. The Board has released a Directive on Automated Decision-Making to ensure that AI-driven decision-making is compatible with core administrative law principles.

One of the central questions in understanding the legal aspects of AI is how the law will evolve in response to it. Will it be through the imposition of new laws and regulations, or will it be through the development of new laws by applying existing laws to new scenarios?

AI has already been used and accepted in a number of US decisions. In Canada, litigation involving AI is in its early stages. For example, a lawsuit involving an AI system has commenced in Quebec, where the owner of Montreal's Galerie NuEdge claimed that a single image from Adam Basanta's project violated her copyright.

Privacy is another significant legal issue that AI users will face. The volume and relativity of data collection raise privacy concerns. Governments worldwide are updating their privacy legislation to respond to these concerns. The GDPR, enacted by the European Parliament, is a comprehensive set of rules designed to keep the personal data of all EU citizens safe from unauthorized access or use. In contrast, US federal lawmakers have been relatively slow to act on privacy concerns.

AI is a complex and rapidly evolving area of law, and its legal and ethical implications are still being understood.

A Critical Thought on AI legal regulation

According to Barrio Andres (2021), AI systems can make tough decisions once reserved for humans. These decisions could range from life and death situations, like using autonomous killer robots in the military, to social and economic issues, such as determining who gets a scholarship or when to grant parole to a prisoner.

The problem is that if humans made these decisions, they would be subject to legal rules and have to explain their actions legally. But when it comes to AI, there are currently no such regulations in place.

To make things worse, the regulation of AI is mostly left to corporate interests and ethical considerations. This can be a problem, as we've seen in the past with the global financial crisis of 2008, which was a result of a self-regulated industry that spiraled out of control.

However, some efforts are being made to regulate AI. For example, DeepMind, a company working on AI, has formed an ethics committee that includes leading public analysts like transhumanist philosopher Nick Bostrom and economist Jeffrey Sachs. The Partnership on AI, a group dedicated to promoting responsible AI, also includes non-profit organizations like the American Civil Liberties Union, Human Rights Watch, and UNICEF.

But here's the thing, ethical frameworks differ from legal frameworks. Legal frameworks can only be developed by international or state legislatures, which have the power to impose sanctions or even prison sentences for non-compliance. Ethical frameworks, on the other hand, are only binding internally and carry spiritual consequences for non-compliance.

Unfortunately, unlike Silicon Valley, most states are still lagging behind in regulating AI. The longer we wait, the more difficult it will be to manage AI's future properly.

Managing Technological and Ethical Issues

You should have already noticed how intelligent machine systems are improving our lives. From optimizing logistics and detecting fraud to composing art and conducting research, these systems are making our world more efficient and richer.

And guess what? Tech giants like Alphabet, Amazon, Facebook, IBM, and Microsoft, along with great minds like Stephen Hawking and Elon Musk, believe that now is the time to talk about the limitless potential of artificial intelligence. This new frontier is just as much about ethics and risk assessment as it is about emerging technology.

There are three main ethical issues related to AI in business that we need to consider:

Bias

Humans are responsible for creating and implementing algorithms and machine learning models that run AI. However, they bring conscious and unconscious biases that can lead to biased outcomes. The data used to train AI models also reflects human biases.

To avoid bias, AI development requires diverse teams and extensive testing. If we fail to do this, AI models can reinforce racial, gender, disability-related, and age-related biases that deepen inequalities and prejudices. For example, Tidio, a tech company, conducted an experiment with AI text-to-image creators that revealed gender bias.

When asked to provide a photo of an ambitious CEO, the

algorithm produced only middle-aged men. When asked to produce a diverse group photo, it generated a photo of mostly white, thin, and all able-bodied people. Such biases can also lead to denied mortgages for people of color and wrongful arrests and interrogations based on AI-driven facial recognition technology.

Privacy

AI relies on vast data sets to train machine learning programs, but this data can come from sources like social media, mobile phones, and other devices. AI tracks every click, view, duration of view, post, keyword search, and the like to build complex profiles on individuals, which can create privacy concerns. AI can also identify patterns in data to make predictions about individuals and groups.

This means AI can discern information about people they don't intend to disclose, using it for purposes users did not consent to. For example, employment recruitment AI may use the information applicants provide to make inferences about their mental health, political persuasion, or likelihood of needing parental leave, which could influence hiring decisions.

Additionally, AI combined with other technologies can create privacy concerns, such as excessive surveillance when AI facial recognition programs are paired with closed-circuit cameras in public spaces.

Manipulation and Deception

Another ethical issue related to AI is its ability to manipulate and deceive. The unethical use of AI can spread disinformation, suppress political views, and create hostile societal divisions. AI can find patterns in people's digital footprints that reveal their interests, motivations, finances, preferences, dislikes, political beliefs, and more.

While businesses may use this information to deliver targeted marketing and personalized services, it can also create manipulative tools that prey on people's weaknesses and guide them toward specific decisions, stripping them of their autonomy. AI can also produce and distribute factually inaccurate content, such as deepfakes, which can influence how people vote, whether they get vaccinations, whom they trust and distrust, and more.

For example, a Chinese government disinformation campaign featuring AI-generated videos that delivered fake stories meant to undermine the United States was recently uncovered by the research firm Graphika. Hackers have also circulated deep fake videos of public figures saying and doing things they didn't say or do, which can completely distort the truth.

So, as AI continues to revolutionize the business world, we must consider these ethical issues and take steps to address them. By doing so, we can ensure that AI is a force for good rather than one that exacerbates biases, violates privacy, and undermines truth.

Planning for Long-term Success

Like many others, you might stumble upon products or services claiming to help you earn significant money online within a short time. Though some success stories exist, the truth is that most people who try to make money online find a different reality.

The more practical approach to building a stable and lucrative online business is to focus on long-term growth instead of quick money-making schemes. An online business built with a long-term approach will provide a solid foundation and a better chance for success.

If you're committed to building a real online business and willing to work, you must adopt a long-term approach rather than relying on gimmicks or shortcuts to earn quick money.

If you're ready to play the long game, here are a few tips for you:

1. Understand Your Target Audience

It's essential to understand your audience before creating

content, promotions, or products that they may or may not want. Take the time to research your target audience and get to know their needs and wants. If you haven't started your site, you can research niche or industry-specific forums to see what people are talking about and what products they respond to.

You can also browse other blogs in the niche and read comments to observe the types of products being promoted. If you already have a site, you can analyze your site's stats to see what type of content attracts the most traffic, which blog posts draw the most comments, and what content is shared the most on social media. You can also survey your readers to get more insight.

2. Choose a Timeless Topic

When choosing a topic for your website, ensure it will be relevant for years. Avoid creating a site around a time-sensitive topic, as it will quickly become outdated, and your audience will drift away. If your site relies on a particular product, topic, or event, and its popularity dries up, your business will suffer. There may be opportunities to make money for a limited time, but it's important to have a long-term focus.

3. Consider Your Target Audience's Lifespan

When targeting your audience, it's essential to consider how long they will remain within your audience range and how quickly they may outgrow your offerings. For example, if you cater to beginner photographers, your content and products should focus on photography fundamentals. However, once they acquire this knowledge, they may no longer require your services.

To prevent losing your audience, you need to provide content that caters to different levels of expertise and divides it into sections based on skill levels. This way, visitors can progress from one section to another as they develop their skills and expertise, making them recurring visitors for longer.

By providing content that caters to your target audience's lifespan, you can retain your audience and avoid the need to continuously attract new visitors to replace those who have outgrown your offerings.

4. Prioritize Long-Term Growth Over Quick Monetary Gains

Avoid sacrificing long-term success for short-term income. Focus on building the trust of your audience and developing a relationship with them instead of looking to make money now. This will take time and effort, but the long-term result is that they will be much more responsive whenever you promote a product as an affiliate or offer your product for sale.

Don't sell banner ads at the most prominent locations on your site, and start making some decent revenue from them.

Instead, use that valuable screen space to encourage visitors to subscribe to your email list. You may not make as much money right now by promoting your email list, but it will be more profitable in the long run.

There are still many more points, but I consider these four to be the foundational points for others.

Chapter Recap

The chapter covers several important aspects of running a successful AI business. First, it emphasizes the need to adapt to changes in the AI market, including new technologies and shifting customer demands. It also discusses the importance of managing cash flow, budgets, and financial risks to ensure the company remains stable and sustainable.

Addressing customer complaints and negative feedback is another key area of focus, as it helps businesses improve their products and services and maintain positive relationships with their customers. The chapter also emphasizes the need to avoid burnout, maintain motivation among team members, and deal with legal and regulatory issues that can arise when operating an AI business.

Managing technological and ethical issues is another important consideration, as AI can have significant societal and ethical implications. Finally, the chapter stresses the importance of planning for long-term success, including developing a strong company culture, building strategic partnerships, and continuously investing in research and development.

Conclusion

After the completion of this book, I went over it again, and I realized that it is a comprehensive book that provides readers with a thorough understanding of artificial intelligence and how it can be used to generate passive income.

The book covers various aspects of AI, including the basics of chatbots, natural language processing, and machine learning, making it a valuable resource for beginners and experienced professionals.

Before using ChatGPT, I stressed the importance of understanding the basics of AI and how it works. This includes learning about the different types of AI, such as supervised and unsupervised learning, and how they are used to develop chatbots. Readers are also given advice on how to choose the right chatbot platform, which is an important consideration when starting an AI-powered side hustle.

The book also covers the topic of AI-powered passive income, which is becoming increasingly popular. Readers are introduced to different ways of generating income using AI, such as building chatbots that can perform tasks, offer customer service, or provide information. I also shared valuable tips on how to monetize AI-powered projects and create a sustainable income stream.

Chapter three provided guidance on getting started with AI-powered side hustles, including the necessary skills and tools to develop and deploy chatbots. Readers are given practical advice on creating chatbots from scratch, including using natural language processing and machine learning. I discussed the importance of setting realistic goals and timelines for AI projects.

To stay ahead of the game, I recommended staying updated with the latest AI trends and technologies in Chapter four. This includes attending conferences, networking with other professionals, and taking online courses to improve one's skills. The book also covers the importance of tracking progress and adjusting AI projects to ensure their success.

Scaling a side hustle is another important topic covered in the book. I discussed various strategies for growing an AI-powered business, such as collaborating with other professionals and leveraging social media and online platforms.

Marketing strategies are another crucial aspect of AI-powered businesses, and the book provided readers with insights into different marketing techniques, including SEO, social media, and email marketing. In chapter seven, I emphasized the importance of creating engaging and interactive content that resonates with the target audience.

Chapter eight covers troubleshooting and problem-solving, essential skills for any AI professional. Readers are given practical advice on identifying and fixing common AI problems, such as chatbots that fail to respond or provide inaccurate information. This chapter also covers issues pertaining to managing financial matters.

Finally, legal and ethical issues related to AI, including data privacy, intellectual property rights, and transparency, were not left out.

In conclusion, this book is a valuable resource for anyone interested in AI-powered, specifically ChatGPT-powered side hustles or looking to develop their skills in the field. The book provides practical advice, useful tips, and real-world examples of how AI—ChatGPT—can generate passive income and create successful businesses.

By following the advice in this book, you can quickly develop the skills and knowledge required to succeed in your side hustle business.

How much value have you gotten from this book? I look forward to reading your testimonials and reviews.

If you enjoyed reading this book, please leave a review on Amazon. Your feedback will help others looking to start learning all about ChatGPT and AI by guiding them toward the right resources. With the right mindset and strategies, anyone can utilize and monetize from the revolutionary artificial intelligence that this world is heavily focusing on to improve the lives and businesses of all around.

References

5 A.I tools to scale online business. (2023, January 19). ImageTranslate Blog. https://www.imagetranslate.com/blog/5-a-i-tools-to-scale-online-business/

Adkuloo, N. (2022, June 12). *8 Ways to Use AI in Email Marketing in 2023*. Mailmodo. https://www.mailmodo.com/guides/ai-in-email-marketing/

AI Ethical Issues in Business | Maryville Online. (2023, March 28). Maryville Online. https://online.maryville.edu/blog/ai-ethical-issues/

Attarbashi, B. H. (n.d). Artificial Intelligence's Impact on the Future of Work | AI Bees. https://www.ai-bees.io/

Author, G. (2021, November 5). *5 Steps to Creating a Growth Strategy that Actually Works*. WordStream. https://www.wordstream.com/blog/ws/2020/10/28/growth-strategy

References

Baker, J. (2021). AI in Sales: How Artificial Intelligence is Changing the Sales Landscape. Inside Big Data. Retrieved from https://insidebigdata.com/2021/02/12/ai-in-sales-how-artificial-intelligence-is-changing-the-sales-landscape/

Barrio Andres, M. (2021, June 23). Towards legal regulation of artificial intelligence. *REVISTA IUS, 15*(48). https://doi.org/10.35487/rius.v15i48.2021.661

Buffini, B. (2022, January 4). *7 Tips to Avoid Burnout When Growing a Business | Entrepreneur*. Entrepreneur. https://www.entrepreneur.com/leadership/7-tips-to-avoid-burnout-when-growing-a-business/404061

Casarella, D., & , Contributor, D. C. (2021, May 4). *The Difference Between Sales and Marketing*. https://www.uschamber.com/co/. https://www.uschamber.com/co/grow/sales/sales-vs-marketing

Columbus, L. (2020). 10 Ways AI Is Revolutionizing Sales. Forbes. Retrieved from https://www.forbes.com/sites/louiscolumbus/2020/01/05/10-ways-ai-is-revolutionizing-sales/?sh=43ef50e36c3a

Desyllas, J. (2022, September 15). *How to Build An Email List: 14 Proven Tactics [2023]*. Email Marketing Automation Platform for Thriving Businesses. https://moosend.com/blog/how-to-build-an-email-list-from-scratch/

Doyle, K. (2023, February 18). AI For Marketing: How (and Why) You Should Build an AI Marketing Strategy. https://www.jasper.ai/blog/ai-for-marketing

Emerging legal issues in an AI-driven world. (n.d.). Lexology. https://www.lexology.com/library/detail.aspx?g=4284727f-3bec-43e5-b230-fad2742dd4fb

Fine, N. (n.d.). *Automating Your Sales Funnel With an AI Sales Assistant.* Vonage. https://www.vonage.com.tw/resources/articles/automating-your-sales-funnel-with-an-ai-sales-assistant/

Gartner. (2020). AI for Sales: The Future of Sales Engagement. https://www.gartner.com/en/sales-service/insights/ai-for-sales

Haricharan, (2022, December 5). *7 Common Mistakes to Avoid for AI in Customer Service*. Saxon. https://saxon.ai/blogs/7-common-mistakes-to-avoid-when-using-ai-in-customer-service/

Hines, K. (2023, May 9). *Microsoft Unveils AI Chat Monetization For Digital Partners*. Search Engine Journal. https://www.searchenginejournal.com/microsoft-unveils-ai-chat-monetization-for-digital-partners/486525/

How Artificial Intelligence will Change Business Forever. (2018, September 14). Apogaeis. https://www.apogaeis.com/blog/how-artificial-intelligence-will-change-business-forever/

How To Avoid Burnout As an Entrepreneur. (2022, May 6). How to Avoid Burnout as an Entrepreneur (2023). https://www.shopify.com/blog/how-to-avoid-burnout

How to Build Your Email List in Less than an Hour | Mailchimp. (n.d.). Mailchimp. https://mailchimp.com/resources/how-to-build-your-email-list/

How to Reduce Cash Flow Risk. (n.d.). How to Reduce Cash Flow Risk | GoCardless. https://gocardless.com/guides/posts/how-to-reduce-cash-flow-risk/

Kissmetrics. (2021). How to Use Artificial Intelligence in Sales: 10 Powerful Examples. https://www.kissmetrics.com/growth/ai-in-sales/

Knight, R. (2015, April 2) *How to Overcome Burnout and Stay Motivated*. Harvard Business Review. https://hbr.org/2015/04/how-to-overcome-burnout-and-stay-motivated

Lewis, A. (2019, June 7). *How to Monetize a Loyal Audience by Selling Digital Products*. Foundr. https://foundr.com/articles/building-a-business/finance/monetize-an-audience

McCormick, K. (n.d.). *39 Ways to Increase Traffic to Your Website - WordStream*. WordStream. https://www.wordstream.com/blog/ws/2014/08/14/increase-traffic-to-my-website

McCormick, K. (n.d.). *6 Ways to Use ChatGPT for Small Business Marketing (+6 Ways NOT to Use It)*. WordStream. https://www.wordstream.com/blog/ws/2023/03/06/how-to-use-chatgpt-for-small-business-marketing

Meltwater. (2021). Competitive Intelligence for Sales: Use AI to Win More Deals. https://www.meltwater.com/en/blog/competitive-intelligence-for-sales-use-ai-to-win-more-deals/

Methvin, A. (2023, January 24). *ChatGPT in Marketing: In-Depth Guide with Tools, Strategies & Examples*. NoGood™: Growth Marketing Agency. https://nogood.io/2023/01/24/chat-gpt-in-marketing/

Mirestean, A., Farias, A., Deodoro, J., Boukherouaa, E. B., AlAjmi, K., Iskender, E., Ravikumar, R., & Shabsigh, G. (2021, October). Powering the Digital Economy: Opportunities and Risks of Artificial Intelligence in Finance. *Departmental Papers*, *2021*(024), 1. https://doi.org/10.5089/9781589063952.087

Mishra, P. (2020, June 3). *How to Use AI for Sales Funnel Optimisation in Your Business*. (2020, June 3). Digital Doughnut. https://www.digitaldoughnut.com/articles/2020/may-2020/how-to-use-ai-for-sales-funnel-optimisation

Nagarajan, M. (2021). 5 Ways AI is Revolutionizing Sales. SalesHacker. https://www.saleshacker.com/how-is-ai-revolutionizing-sales/

Panel®, E. (2021, June 21). *Council Post: 16 Best Tips For Crafting A Successful Growth Strategy Plan*. Forbes. https://www.forbes.com/sites/forbesbusinessdevelopmentcouncil/2021/06/21/16-best-tips-for-crafting-a-successful-growth-strategy-plan/

References

Patricia, C. *How do you keep up with the latest trends and innovations in AI?* (2023, April 27). Six Tips to Keep up With AI Trends and Innovations. https://www.linkedin.com/advice/3/how-do-you-keep-up-latest-trends-innovations-7041842070671556608

Phillips, B. (2022, Ma7 17). *How AI is Changing Customer Complaint Management | NICE.* https://www.nice.com:443/blog/how-ai-is-changing-how-companies-handle-customer-complaints

Rahal, A. (2020, August 31). *Council Post: Negative Feedback: Four Examples Of Negative Feedback Online And How To Deal With It.* Forbes. https://www.forbes.com/sites/theyec/2020/08/31/negative-feedback-four-examples-of-negative-feedback-online-and-how-to-deal-with-it/

Schunemann, C. (n.d.). *Budget Forecasting and How to Make a Budget Forecast | Layer Blog.* Layer Blog. https://blog.golayer.io/finance/what-is-budget-forecasting

Sood, R. (2020). The Future of AI in Sales: What Salespeople Need to Know. SalesHacker. https://www.saleshacker.com/the-future-of-ai-in-sales/

Staff, E. (2023, February 16). *How Can Marketers Use ChatGPT? Here Are the Top 11 Uses. | Entrepreneur.* Entrepreneur. https://www.entrepreneur.com/science-technology/how-can-marketers-use-chatgpt-here-are-the-top-11-uses/445015

Start Monetizing Your Marketing Activities: Turning AI into ROI. (n.d.). Start Monetizing Your Marketing Activities: Turning AI Into ROI. https://www.appier.com/en/resources/start-monetizing-your-marketing-activities

Susanna. (2022, August 31). *How to monetize your audience (learnings from 60K+ creators).* Sellfy Blog. https://blog.sellfy.com/audience-monetization/

Threecolts: Six Ways AI Can Boost Your E-Commerce Business. (2023, May 3). Threecolts: Six Ways AI Can Boost Your E-Commerce Business. https://www.threecolts.com/blog-articles/six-ways-ai-boost-e-commerce-business

Vecchio, L. D. (2020, June 11). *Cash Flow Risk In Business and How To Reduce It | Planergy Software.* Planergy Software. https://planergy.com/blog/cash-flow-risk/

Vidakovic, I. (2022, October 21). 8 Effective Ways to Use AI in Email Marketing. https://textcortex.com/post/8-effective-ways-to-use-ai-in-email-marketing

What are Backlinks? And How to Build Them in 2023. (n.d.). Backlinko. https://backlinko.com/hub/seo/backlinks

What are the benefits and challenges of using AI for budget forecasting? (2023, April 27). AI For Budget Forecasting: Pros and Cons. https://www.linkedin.com/advice/3/what-benefits-challenges-using-ai-budget-forecasting

Zhel, M. (2023, April 19). *What is a Sales Funnel? And How To Build One in 2023.* Mailmunch. https://www.mailmunch.com/blog/sales-funnel

Other Sources

https://www.pinterest.com/pin/a-motivational-side-hustle-quote-from-forbes--250090585549800789/

https://www.forbes.com/sites/sap/2013/01/16/22-best-marketing-quotes-to-drive-your-marketing-strategy/?sh=2ad2e1767e06

https://www.thesuccessfulspirit.com/quotes-about-artificial-intelligence/